GOLDEN R<

Golden Rabbit

David Ashworth

This book is dedicated to:

Harriët Kroon,
Eve and Tilda.

On mid-winter's evening 2014
they called me on Skype
from The Netherlands.

Tilda said, 'Tell us a story.'
'Yes, tell us a story,' said Eve.

Golden Rabbit is that story.

Such is the way the Universe brings creation into the world.

Sometimes through the request of angels, fairies and sprites;
and sometimes through the request of girls.

Contents

Mid-winter's Eve, 2014

The old wizard sat by the log fire in his little cottage at the edge of the ancient woodland. He was watching the wild movement of the branches and listening to the sounds of the cold, winter wind howling through the trees. It was a dark, bitter night in the borderlands of old Wales and Shropshire. No stars were shining from the heavens and the spirit of the wind was whispering that snow was on the way.

He rose from his armchair to put another log on the fire and then sat down again. Suddenly, the sound of the crackling wood was broken by a ding-a-ling-a-ling. It was Skype calling on the computer. Oh yes, we still have wizards in the modern age, but we often don't know who they are. They blend between worlds, appearing as ordinary people to those who don't yet have the open heart to feel the light that they carry.

'Who do you think that could be?' said the wizard to Conejo, the old Spanish rabbit who lived with him in the cottage. 'You better answer it.'

'But I'm toasting my ears by the fire,' said the rabbit.

'Well it's your turn to get up,' the wizard replied.

'Oh, very well,' said Conejo.

The rabbit got up and flicked his whiskers to make sure they were straight and presentable. He cleared his throat to speak his best English, which wasn't really very good at all, but what can you expect from an old Spanish rabbit?

Skype opened up and it was Angel from the east with two young girls who came to stay with her every now and then.

'Olaaa,' said the rabbit joyfully. He was so glad that he had answered Skype now, as Angel was one of his favourite people.

'Hello Conejo,' said Angel. 'How are you?'

'Sí, I am very fine, gracias, muchos gracias and gracias again Señora, and how are your feathers? Do they keep you warm at a time like this when the wind is howling from the east and snow on its way?'

'Well Conejo, you mean my wings, not my feathers,' Angel replied.

'Sí, sí. I mean your wings, sí, wings.'

The rabbit tended to repeat everything because he liked to hear his own voice speaking in English.

'Only a few people can see my wings, Conejo, as they are hidden from most eyes. You can see them, and the animals and nature spirits can see them, but for those who can't I look just like any other human being. In this lifetime, my feathers are so fine that they are not very warm at all and so I have to wear clothes of the finest wool, spun by the spirits of the sacred sheep. That is how I keep warm when the winter is getting as cold as it is now.'

'Ah sí, sí,' said Conejo. 'I remember that only those of us with the inner sight can see your hidden beauty and magnificence. Your secret life, sí, sí.'

Meanwhile, the two girls were so surprised to see a talking rabbit that they couldn't say anything at all, and now the rabbit was even blowing kisses to them all. Angel blew kisses back to Conejo. Then the girls blew kisses as this seemed to be the way that talking rabbits greeted people.

Conejo looked at the girls and said to Angel, 'Who are these lovely young Sprites?'

'They are not Sprites,' said Angel, 'they are —'

Conejo cut in. 'I know, I know, don't tell me. You have brought with you on this cold and windy night a couple of beautiful flower fairies to protect them from the chilly, snow-filled winds.'

'No Conejo,' Angel laughed. 'This is Eve and this is Tilda and they are girls.'

'You mean girls like they have in the mortal world?' asked Conejo.

'Yes, that is right Conejo, real, proper girls.'

'Well, I never,' exclaimed the Rabbit. 'What do they do? What do they eat? What do they say?'

'Do they eat rabbits? Do they shout and make a noise? Do they sing words of old songs that make a rabbit's ears painful?'

'What…, what…, what on earth are girls for?'

Conejo finally finished his stream of excited questions with a quizzical look on his face and his head on one side, as clearly he didn't understand girls. He then ran round in three circles before looking at them all again.

Angel laughed and the girls laughed too.

Angel said, 'Well they are not for anything unusual or out of the ordinary, they are just…'

'They just are what?' cut in Conejo.

'They are just girls,' she finished.

'Well, I think I better sit down and rest,' said the rabbit. 'This is all a bit too much for my furry ears to understand. Girls just are … are just … is just … just is … is just confusing to an old Spanish rabbit?'

Conejo stepped away from the screen and lay down in front of the log fire. Angel and the girls could hear him mumbling to himself, 'Well, I'll toast my ears and then I might understand. Sí, sí, I'll toast my ears.'

Then he shouted to the wizard, 'Dabeith!'

'Dabeith, you had better come to the magic window and speak with Angel and these girls. I am not sure what they want, but I am sure that I need to toast my ears again before I become too confused. Oh dear, I think I must be an old rabbit now. It's all too much. It's all too much.'

The Emptiness

The old wizard looked into the magic window, as Conejo called it, sat back in his chair and stroked his chin.

'Well, hello and how are you all on this mid-winter's eve? Tomorrow the sun will rise and begin to travel to the north again, bringing firstly chill winds and snow, but at the same time more light. It is the time that light returns to us.'

Tilda said, 'Tell us a story.'

'Yes, tell us a story,' said Eve.

'A story,' said the wizard. 'You want a story, hmm, well, let me see.'

'I could tell you about all the magic in the wood, or the elves that guard the oak trees; or how the clouds and the trees speak to each other – or indeed, a thousand stories of the fairy folk and the real world just beyond this one where we are speaking now. Which will it be?'

Conejo responded from by his warm fire. 'Don't tell them a story, tell them about the rabbit.'

The wizard looked round and said, 'Which rabbit do you mean, Conejo?'

'The Golden Rabbit. Tell them about the Golden Rabbit that lives in our wood.'

'Oh yes, that is a good idea. Thank you, Conejo. Now girls, are you ready?' said the wizard.

The girls nodded that they were.

'Once upon a time...Oh yes, you have to begin a story that way,' the old wizard laughed. 'Once upon a time, there was nothing. That's right, nothing, just the black night of emptiness and nothing else. Not even an earth to stand upon. Then there was a flash of light so intense that it lit up the whole of this great emptiness. Rocks were flying everywhere and some of these rocks were as big as the earth. In fact, one of them would become the earth.'

The wizard clapped his hands and waved his arms about.

'Bang! Crash! Light and rocks everywhere, flying through space. If you want to see what it was like, throw a pebble into still water very hard and imagine that was the flash of light and the great boom. Then watch all the tiny water droplets flying everywhere and imagine they were the rocks flying through space. Ha! Just like that. Caboom!'

'Can you imagine how exciting that must have been for the emptiness? All of a sudden there was light, and it was everywhere at the same time. Next time you go outside at night, if there are no clouds you can see all the billions of pin-points of light in the darkness and each one is full of magic.'

'The scientists are always trying to understand the magic of the light out there, but sometimes they are not even as smart as a rabbit, because some rabbits know where to find the light on earth, and I bet hardly any scientists have ever seen it. But you girls can be the smartest in the world if you listen to the Golden Rabbit and learn what she teaches. Then you can be real scientists and show the older scientists what they missed, hahaha!'

'Oh, I mustn't get too excited,' said the wizard. 'The last time I told this story, which was a long time ago, I actually knocked some planets out of the sky when I was waving my arms about. Oh yes, mustn't get too excited,' he chuckled as he remembered the chaos that he had created.

The Golden Rabbit

It was very early one morning, before people were up for school and work and the furry little bunnies were peeping out of the edge of the wood to see if it was safe to come into the garden and nibble some grass. Rabbits come out early so that nobody can see their secrets; but back in the old days even the bunnies didn't know they had secrets until one day a light appeared in the wood.

The light glowed golden as it moved gently and silently towards the edge of the wood where the bunnies were nipping in and out of the sunlight playing. The older rabbits were eating quietly. Suddenly they all stopped what they were doing and stood totally still. They looked back into the dusky wood where they saw the glow of a golden light. What is that, they thought? They looked at each other uncertain what to do. Slowly and gently the light became brighter and began to take form. At this, some of the bunnies panicked and ran for their burrows – as rabbits do. As the light increased it took the form of a huge rabbit. A great Golden Rabbit. She was sitting quite still and the golden light was pouring out of her, lighting up the dark woodland.

The bunnies who remained were very still, not knowing what to do. There was only one way to safety and that was back into the wood but this glowing Golden Rabbit was just sitting there looking at them. The bunnies looked at each other and then back into the wood to see the Golden Rabbit slowly hopping away from them.

They were now feeling safe again but one bunny hopped a few steps towards the light in the wood, following the footsteps of the Golden Rabbit. One at a time the other bunnies followed, whilst the older rabbits raised their heads to watch.

At this moment most of their fear had left them. As the Golden Rabbit moved gently into the wood, wherever her feet touched the ground there was a patch of golden light. These glowed for a moment and then faded but it was like she was laying down a pathway to follow. A Path of Light.

Presently, she passed beneath the great oaks and under an old holly bush, stepping out into a little circle of bright green grass lit by the morning sun. She turned and sat down and her light expanded to fill the glade.

The bunnies came to the edge of the glade and peered through the tall grass and leaves, looking at this Golden Rabbit.

The Golden Rabbit put her lips to the grass and began to nibble. This is a rabbit sign that all is safe. The bunnies saw that her whiskers lit up and glowed golden too. As the light increased around the Golden Rabbit the bunnies became more excited, and then one of them took a big leap and hopped into the beautiful green circle, looking right at the Golden Rabbit.

At this sudden leap all the other bunnies became full of fear again and lay down low so that they couldn't be seen, their ears flat against their backs.

The Golden Rabbit was four times bigger than the little bunny who now sat before her. Golden Rabbit was sitting right at the centre of the grassy circle and looked deeply into the eyes of the little bunny.

'Hello Rahh,' she said.

'You are wondering how I know your name.'

'I know it because I know everything. I know who you are and I know who sent you here, to this lovely safe woodland. I know because I come from a place that is full of light and the light shows me anything I want to see. Today I came to see you, Rahh,' said the Golden Rabbit.

Little Rahh sat totally still, wishing now that he had not

jumped into the circle but he hadn't been able to prevent it from happening. It was like his body just leaped in by itself.

Golden Rabbit looked at Rahh and spoke again.

'Do not be afraid little bunny for you will go on a great journey from this day forth. You will become one of the greatest rabbits ever to walk upon the mother earth because I will show you a secret that will fill you with light.'

'All other rabbits will be aware of you and some will even be wary of you, but all of them will know that you are different from the rest.'

The other bunnies were listening as they lay low in the long, cool grass. Golden Rabbit looked over Rahh's head towards them and said, 'It is safe. You may step into the circle of light.'

One at a time they each crawled forward on their bellies, not brave enough to stand up taller than Rahh, and they all stayed behind him too.

Golden Rabbit looked at them all in turn but they could not look into her eyes as her light was so bright. All the bunnies looked down towards the earth, except Rahh, who was still looking directly into her eyes.

She took a step forward and said to Rahh, 'Show me your courage.'

Rahh did not know what she meant but he continued to look into her eyes. Suddenly, he felt a strange feeling inside, like he was growing, as if he was becoming bigger within. He looked at his furry bunny feet and they twitched and then one foot moved forward, towards Golden Rabbit. Then the other and then his back feet, and then he stood up on all four feet in front of her.

'Why do you stand in front of me, Rahh?' asked Golden Rabbit.

'I don't know,' said Rahh. 'I had a strange feeling inside and my feet began to move towards you.'

'That feeling is your heart,' said Golden Rabbit.

[8]

'Your courage is in your heart and it is reaching out to the light that is inside me. That is why your name is Rahh, because you have the courage of the lion and your heart shines like the Great Light in the blue. You are filled with light, but it is not yet awakened and shining. It is now time for your heart to grow, and that is what you felt inside. Your heart just grew, and with it, your courage grew.'

'That is why I have come to the wood today, to illuminate your heart, Rahh.'

Golden Rabbit looked at the other bunnies and said to them, 'You are all special, all of you, but your hearts are still a little afraid of the light and so you were afraid to look into my eyes. You were afraid that my heart might touch you.'

'I will leave you all now, but tomorrow morning, as the Great Light rises into the blue, I will come back to this circle. Those of you who are ready to learn my secrets will be here, because your courage will have grown during the dark time in your burrow. Those of you who are not yet ready will play at the edge of the wood as always.'

The Golden Rabbit looked again into Rahh's eyes, then turned and hopped out of the glade and into the dusk of the woodland without another word.

The bunnies all sat up and looked at Rahh, as if waiting for him to say something. He looked back at them and could see that he was now different from them: they were still innocent and wanting to rush away to nibble the grass, but something had changed inside him.

Smiling at them, Rahh said, 'Come, let us go back to the green grass and continue to eat breakfast.'

There were smiles all around and whiskers bristled into the air as this was what the bunnies really wanted to hear, and Rahh knew it.

4

I am Alone

The following morning before the Great Light rose into the blue, there was a golden glow in the wood. There was peace and stillness and a strange feeling in the air.

The bunnies began to rise and peep out of their burrows, their whiskers twitching in the cool air. Rahh lay in his bed. He was not in a hurry to see the world today. He knew that there was something special for him and he didn't need to rush for it. He knew exactly when he had to move.

The bunnies left the burrow and hopped and skipped around and then made their way to the edge of the wood. When Rahh came out of the burrow, none of them were there. They had not even noticed that Rahh was not with them.

Rahh took a few steps towards the edge of the wood where he could see the other bunnies running and hopping. They would nibble a few blades of juicy green grass before rushing back to safety, then out again bouncing happily in the rising light.

Rahh watched carefully. It was like every other day for the bunnies. Nothing had changed. He felt a sadness in his heart for them. Then he suddenly felt alone. He knew that they had already forgotten him on this bright spring morning. As he sat and felt the pain inside him, he heard a faint calling in his furry ears. 'Rahh, it is your time.'

Rahh turned his head and looked deep into the wood; he could feel the calling of the light that was glowing there. It was such a hard decision for him. He loved his brothers and sisters and their happy life together on the edge of the wood, but he knew that he could only go one way from here – into the darkness of the wood.

As he watched the bunnies running and laughing and the Great Light rose higher into the blue, the pain he had felt grew inside him. A tear tumbled down his fur and onto his paw. He looked down and a feeling of great loss washed over him. A thought suddenly filled his tiny head. 'I am alone in this world.' He shook his paw and the tear fell to the earth where it sparkled brightly for a second before disappearing. He turned his back to the Great Light in the blue and his brothers and sisters playing. He felt totally alone but he knew he had no choice. He lifted his head slightly and hopped slowly into the darkness of the deep, deep wood.

He followed the pull in his heart, beginning his search for that small green glade where the great Golden Rabbit had spoken to them all the previous day.

5

Becoming

As Rahh hopped slowly through the wood, he could see the glow of golden light in the distance. He took his time. It was as if he was leaving his old life behind and beginning a new one. He still felt alone, but not desolate or deserted. Somehow he was alone, but not on his own – he couldn't quite explain the feeling.

Golden Rabbit was waiting in the glade when Rahh hopped into the circle of light. She could see the water in his eyes.

'Is it painful, Rahh?' asked Golden Rabbit. 'Does it hurt inside?'

'Yes,' said Rahh. 'Why do I hurt so much? What is happening to me?'

Golden Rabbit replied, 'You are Becoming.'

'What am I becoming?' he asked.

'You are becoming filled with light; and as the light emerges from deep within your heart, the pain can be terrible.'

'With all things that are born, there is a struggle. Look at the flitterflind as it struggles free of the chrysalis. Look at the leaf as it struggles free of the bud. Look at the Great Light in the blue, as it struggles to rise each morning, birthing a new dawn. All things that are born must first struggle,' said Golden Rabbit.

'But I am already born,' puzzled Rahh.

'Yes,' said Golden Rabbit. 'Your body and mind are born, but your heart is now in the struggle of awakening. It is being born at a higher level. You are feeling the pain of the inner struggle, of letting go of the things that you know, like your brothers and sisters and your way of life in the garden on the edge of this wood. You are struggling to let go of the certainty that the garden is always there for you when you eat the sweet breakfast grass.'

'When the child of a two-legged is born, it leaves one world – a dark, warm, watery world inside the belly of a mother – and enters another world; this light and changeable world of the earth mother. It is a complete transformation from naked beauty to a world where others clothe it with all manner of ideas that are not of itself. But even then, the light in the centre of them is not yet born. That struggle is yet to come.'

Golden Rabbit continued, 'You will come to understand, little bunny, that as the light awakens in your centre you will marvel at what you will become. You are safe. You stand within the circle of my light and have been chosen by a light far greater than I to make this journey. I am just your guide.'

'Come closer, Rahh.'

Rahh hopped closer and Golden Rabbit touched his toes with her paw where his tear had fallen. Rahh felt a wave of something warm pass through him and his inner pain dissolved. He suddenly felt freer than ever before, and more than that, suddenly he had no rabbit fear at all.

His ears twitched, his whiskers lifted upwards and he was filled with joy. He looked up to see Golden Rabbit looking deeply into his eyes. He could feel this special feeling growing inside him.

Golden Rabbit asked, 'How do you feel, Rahh?'

'I feel like I am being filled up with something warm, but I don't know what it is. All my pain has gone. It is very sweet, like eating a breakfast of early summer grass, but even sweeter. But I am not sure what this feeling is.'

'It is called love,' said Golden Rabbit. 'You are being filled with love.'

Rahh kept looking at Golden Rabbit, and her eyes continued to fill him with this warm feeling.

'Are you ready to follow me, Rahh?' asked Golden Rabbit.

'I am ready,' he replied.

Golden Rabbit smiled at the little bunny, then turned and hopped out of the glade of bright light and into the cooler shades of the deeper wood. Rahh followed her.

6

Beginning to See

Golden Rabbit took Rahh down a path he had never seen before and it was full of twists and turns and surprises: creatures that were new to him, plants and trees he'd never come across. It was as if everything was brighter in colour too. Everything seemed new, untouched; full of a beauty that touched him inside.

They came to the edge of the wood. The Great Light was rising higher into the blue and Golden Rabbit bent low and passed beneath the fence leading into the field. She turned her back to the sun and asked Rahh to stand next to her.

Golden Rabbit said, 'Look carefully Rahh at where my whiskers point and tell me what you see.'

Golden Rabbit lowered her ears and her whiskers pointed straight ahead. Rahh looked and looked but couldn't see anything.

'I can't see anything,' said Rahh.

'Look again,' Golden Rabbit instructed.

Rahh looked and looked and still he could not see anything.

'I still can't see anything,' said Rahh.

Golden Rabbit laughed and said again, 'Tell me what you see. You must be able to see something.'

'Well, I can see the green breakfast grass and that is all. Oh and the blue above, and if I look behind me, I can see the Great Light too.'

'Very good, that's right Rahh,' said Golden Rabbit, 'You can actually see many things if you look carefully and think about it, but most beings don't think too much. They don't look properly. They don't observe, they don't question, they don't understand

and most importantly, they don't see what is in front of them.'

'Most importantly for you today, we are going to look at the grass. You can see the grass, Rahh, and what is the grass sitting upon?'

'It is sitting upon the earth,' said Rahh.

Smiling, Golden Rabbit asked, 'Does the grass just sit there, then?'

'No,' said Rahh, 'It grows.'

'That's right,' said Golden Rabbit. 'The grass grows upon the earth. So, now your sight and understanding of truth is developing. You are learning how to see. A few moments ago you could see nothing and now you can see that the grass is growing on the earth.'

'How does the grass help you, Rahh?' said Golden Rabbit.

'Help me?' questioned Rahh.

'Yes Rahh. How does the grass help you?'

Rahh was very thoughtful. He suddenly felt important because this morning he was learning how to think and see things in a new way.

'I think it helps me because I can take it into my burrow and make a soft bed to lie on, but most importantly I can eat it when it is juicy and wet in the morning and I feel very happy inside afterwards.'

'You are becoming, Rahh. You are becoming very thoughtful and your mind is developing, which is very good and a great sign that one day you will be a great rabbit. You have worked very hard this morning and we haven't even eaten breakfast yet. I will now help you to see some more important things,' said Golden Rabbit.

Rahh remained silent, watching Golden Rabbit.

Golden Rabbit put her paw in front of her on the grass and said, 'This is your grass, Rahh. It is also your life.'

Rahh's eyes lit up. Golden Rabbit could feel his burning questions coming and she put a paw to her whiskers to indicate that Rahh should remain quiet.

She continued. 'The grass is your life, Rahh, for without the grass you would have no breakfast each morning, as the Great Light rises into the blue.'

'The grass is fed by your mother, the brown earth, which is rich in food for the green grass.'

'The Great Light in the blue brings forth the light of your father, which shines down upon the tiny seed of grass and wakes it up. The moisture in the mornings helps it to grow and the mother feeds it with all the nutrients from the leaves of the trees that have fallen in the passing season of light before we enter the cold burrowing time.'

Golden Rabbit stopped for a moment. She looked deeply at Rahh, watching him taking all this amazing new information into his life. Then she continued.

'The grass is full of your mother and father and each nibble you take of a single blade of grass feeds you, makes your tummy full, helps to make you happy, but most importantly it helps you to grow.'

'All the nutrients that make the grass grow then make your muscles strong, your eyesight keen and healthy, and your bones solid so that you are a happy, healthy rabbit who can play a part in the great game of life.'

Rahh was thoughtful and then said, 'I never really noticed that the grass fed me and helped me to grow. I thought it was just a fun thing to do when coming out of the burrow after the dark time and then eating until you can't eat any more.'

Golden Rabbit said, 'I could tell you a hundred more things that you cannot yet see with your sight as it is right now, Rahh. Most of the beings on the earth are the same. They live in a very simple way, which is good and fine, but one day they will need to wake up and see things in their true light; otherwise, there will be a great disaster in all burrows of the earth.'

Golden Rabbit smiled at Rahh and her whiskers curled up a bit, which showed that she was very happy that Rahh's eyes were opening and he was seeing things in truth for the first time.

'Now, Rahh, let us eat some breakfast grass together and hop in and out of the wood and run in the sunshine. Would you like that?'

'Yes please,' said Rahh. I would love that. I am very hungry now. I have not eaten any breakfast grass this morning and now the Great Light is high in the blue.'

Rahh began to hop, then run and leap in the air kicking his legs out behind him. After stretching his fur and flicking his whiskers at the blue, he brought his lips to the fresh, green grass and began to nibble.

Golden Rabbit bathed him in her light and watched over him. She was here to guide him but Rahh didn't really understand this yet.

Later, as the Great Light in the blue began to fall back towards the earth, Rahh was very content. He had run and played, eaten his fill and rested in the warmth of the Great Light. Now it was time to leave this new field, but Rahh was suddenly a little worried. He wondered where he would sleep as the dark time came.

'Golden Rabbit,' said Rahh with some alarm in his voice.

'Yes,' said Golden Rabbit.

'Where will I sleep when the dark time comes?'

'As the pale lady light rises to grace the dark time, you will be safe Rahh. You will sleep in a new burrow that I have prepared for you. We will go there now. It is not far, just beyond the field and into the wood. Follow me.'

Golden Rabbit turned and hopped towards the fence and Rahh followed.

Rahh felt relieved, but still a little uncertain. He was going to a strange burrow and he was not sure how this would feel.

7

The Crossroads

Rahh slept deep and well that night, but he missed his brothers and sisters next to him. He missed the warmth of their bodies when they all curled up together. Yet there was another kind of warmth in the burrow that he didn't recognise and it was very comforting. Somehow he knew that he was not alone, even though Golden Rabbit was sleeping somewhere else.

When dawn came, Rahh was still asleep in his dreamy rabbit world until he heard a voice drifting through the misty scenes of eating sweet, wet grass.

'Are you hungry, Rahh?' called Golden Rabbit into Rahh's burrow.

There was no reply as Rahh was in such a deep dream.

Golden Rabbit blew through her whiskers and made a lovely whistling sound. Still there was no reply. Then she shouted down the burrow once more. 'Rahh, are you ready for breakfast?'

'Oh, oh … er yes, I am awake. I think I may be hungry, I'm not sure,' said Rahh, as he crawled slowly towards the light at the mouth of his burrow.

'Good morning Rahh,' said Golden Rabbit as he finally popped his head out of the burrow.

'Good morning Golden Rabbit,' said Rahh. 'Is it very early?'

'No, it is normal getting up time,' said Golden Rabbit, 'but I expect you slept deeply in your new burrow.'

'Yes,' said Rahh. 'It was a very deep and warm sleep and I was dreaming of eating lovely, sweet, wet early-morning grass. The sweetest grass that I ever tasted.'

'Ah yes,' laughed Golden Rabbit, 'So you were hungry in your dream and already eating breakfast before you were awake! I think you need to eat something first thing, Rahh,' she went on, 'and so you can lead me to the sweetest grass in the wood and we will break the fast together.'

'What does 'break the fast' mean?' asked Rahh.

'When you don't eat for a certain length of time, it is called fasting. You have not eaten since last evening and so during the night you have fasted. Now you will finish the fasting or break the fast. That is where the name for the first meal of the day comes from. Break-Fast, or breakfast,' explained Golden Rabbit.

'Oh,' said Rahh, his head still dizzy with sleep and one ear flopped over his left eye, 'I didn't see that before.'

'No,' said Golden Rabbit, 'that is just a little something else you did not see, because you did not think about your words and what they really mean. Truth is often right in front of us, but nobody sees it. So, the discussion of Break-Fast is a good lesson first thing in the morning.'

'Now then, lead on Rahh, you can find for our breakfast the sweetest grass in the wood,' said Golden Rabbit.

'But I don't know where it is,' said Rahh.

'Are you hungry?' asked Golden Rabbit.

'Yes,' said Rahh.

'Then follow your heart to some good, sweet food.'

'How do you do that?' asked Rahh.

'Feel the truth of what you need. Just set off and follow the feelings of what you need in your heart, asking your heart for guidance to some good, sweet food.'

'I will try,' said Rahh, and he set off hopping slowly into the woods.

He followed what he thought was his heart, but arrived at a dead end by a stinking pond where all the vegetation was rotting and almost nothing lived. There was a terrible foul smell, which turned his stomach and he certainly didn't want to eat anything near here.

'Pooh,' said Rahh, 'I don't think this is the right place to find good, sweet food.'

Golden Rabbit laughed so that Rahh didn't feel too bad about it.

'You are right, Rahh. How right you are! There is nothing here that is sweet to eat. I think you need to try again.'

'Yes, I think I will go in this other direction.'

Off went the rabbits again, Rahh leading the way and Golden Rabbit a few steps behind him.

'Rahh,' said Golden Rabbit, 'remember to ask your heart to guide you through your feelings.'

'Thank you Golden Rabbit. I am asking, but I'm not sure I am getting an answer.'

Golden Rabbit was blowing through her whiskers to make a lovely little tune to seek breakfast by.

Rahh began to talk to himself, thinking that this might be the way to feel what he was looking for.

'I'll go this way and then I'll turn here and go that way,' he murmured.

As they continued on their journey they eventually came to the edge of a great hole where a tree had been blown over in the winter gales. The pathway was totally blocked and all around were thick brambles that would easily tear a rabbit's lovely fur. Rahh thought that they had better be very careful.

He felt trapped and looked sadly at Golden Rabbit. 'I am very sorry,' he said. 'We cannot continue on this path. We will have to turn back.'

'I have led us to a place where we cannot pass,' said Rahh.

'You are doing very well, Rahh,' said Golden Rabbit. 'You led the way like a good mountain guide.'

Rahh answered. 'But we almost fell into this great big hole and if we had, we would never have been able to climb out again.'

'That is so,' said Golden Rabbit, 'but we didn't fall into the hole, and therefore 'almost' is a useless word to describe our position.'

'We walked through the wood and we stopped when the hole appeared. If we had been walking with our eyes closed, then we might have fallen into the hole, but, unlike many of the two-leggeds, we were walking with our eyes open,' said Golden Rabbit, chuckling to herself at the thought of humans walking around completely disconnected from the truth of what lies within them.

'Rahh, you still led the way. That was incredibly brave: to lead the way into a place that you did not know, such as this huge woodland filled with dark and unknown places,' said Golden Rabbit.

'What shall I do now?' asked Rahh.

Golden Rabbit replied, 'We will have to turn back and find another way. Are you ready to lead again, Rahh?'

Rahh felt uncomfortable; twice he had let Golden Rabbit down and they had still not found the good, sweet grass for breakfast. And now he was very, very hungry indeed.

'What is it that troubles you, little bunny?' said Golden Rabbit.

'I have failed twice to find food for our breakfast and it makes me feel very bad.'

'You did not fail,' said Golden Rabbit. 'You are learning. Each step you take down a learning path, you will most definitely learn something. There is no such thing as failure. There are only learning experiences, Rahh.'

'Even if you give up altogether, you will have learned many things on this short journey, so don't ever think that you failed.

'It is through having the courage to have a go that we eventually achieve what we set out to, and then that would be a totally successful learning experience rather than a partially successful learning experience. So, are you ready to try again, Rahh?'

Feeling a little better, Rahh said, 'Yes, I am ready to try and lead again, Golden Rabbit.'

'Off you go then, Rahh,' said Golden Rabbit. 'I will be right behind you.'

Rahh said, 'We will have to go back the way we came, as there is no way out here.'

'Yes, that's right Rahh, but when you feel the right direction you can then follow the feeling to the sweet grass. Put your nose in the air and let your whiskers sense the moisture of wet morning grass,' said Golden Rabbit.

'Thank you Golden Rabbit.'

Rahh set off and Golden Rabbit followed on, humming a little tune to herself. She was not angry with Rahh at all and wanted him to feel better about himself, and so she hummed a lovely soft tune to lift his spirits and show that she was, in fact, very happy.

Rahh came to a place where different animal tracks were crossing. There were many scents. Striped heads, foxes, sliverers, feathered gages ... and even two-leggeds.

'I am confused,' said Rahh. 'I don't know which way to go. There are too many paths and they are all leading in different directions. I am sorry Golden Rabbit, but I do not know what to do or which way to go, and I am very, very hungry.'

'Sit down for a moment Rahh,' said Golden Rabbit, smiling at him. 'Indeed, you are at a crossroads and you have become confused.'

She waved her foot across the ground and suddenly there was a patch of lovely, sweet grass. 'Look what is right under your nose, Rahh.'

Rahh looked down and was amazed to see lovely, sweet-looking grass. It made his tummy churn as he was so hungry.

'Eat, Rahh,' said Golden Rabbit. 'Then when your tummy has a little joy within, we will speak about this crossroads that you have arrived at.'

Rahh was so grateful that he nibbled the grass and felt the lush wetness on his dry lips, and for a moment he forgot that they were completely lost and that he had no idea which way the path lay.

8

Finding the Path

Rahh finished his breakfast and then again realised they were lost. He felt very guilty and did not wish to speak. He wanted to go down a burrow and hide.

Golden Rabbit had continued to hum her happy tune and occasionally nibble some grass. She was not as hungry as Rahh.

'How sweet was your breakfast, Rahh?' asked Golden Rabbit.

This question distracted him from his uncomfortable thoughts for a moment.

'Oh, it was quite lovely, Golden Rabbit,' he answered. 'It was so sweet, I don't think that I have ever tasted grass so sweet before. And it was all the way out here in the middle of nowhere, beneath the trees of the dark wood.' Then he remembered again that they were lost.

Rahh spoke quietly. 'Golden Rabbit,' he said.

'Yes Rahh.'

'I think we are lost. There are all these paths, and all these different animal smells and I don't know which way to go.'

'No Rahh,' said Golden Rabbit. 'We are not lost at all.'

'Oh, but I think we are,' said Rahh. 'I have taken many paths since the Great Light rose into the blue and I have no idea where we are.'

'No, we are not lost,' laughed Golden Rabbit, and then Rahh had to laugh too.

The rabbits laughed together for a few moments and Rahh felt a little better because he knew that Golden Rabbit was not angry.

When they stopped laughing together, Golden Rabbit said, 'Well, what are we going to do, Rahh?'

Rahh said, 'I don't know which path to take, but you said that we are not lost, Golden Rabbit.'

'That is right, Rahh. WE are not lost – but YOU are!' and she laughed again.

Rahh did not think this was very funny now. He repeated Golden Rabbit's words. 'We are not lost, but YOU are.'

He hung his head low and said to himself, 'I am lost and I don't know which path to take.'

He looked at Golden Rabbit then, and with a hopeful smile on his face said, 'So do you know the way, Golden Rabbit?'

'Yes, I know MY way Rahh, but YOU are lost.'

Rahh was now very puzzled. His full tummy of sweet breakfast grass was now feeling a bit sour and he was confused again.

'Look over there,' said Golden Rabbit, pointing with her nose. 'There is a patch of sunlight on the grass through the trees. Let us go there and sit for a while and see what we can learn about finding our way.'

Rahh was very pleased to hear this suggestion. The rabbits hopped into the sunlight and Rahh sat in front of Golden Rabbit. He saw how majestic she was. She was almost brighter than the Great Light in the blue that shone over their heads and created this warm earth that they were sitting on. She was very beautiful, he thought.

Golden Rabbit said, 'There is only one path, Rahh.'

'But I saw many paths,' he puzzled.

'Yes, all rabbits can see many paths, but there is only one path for YOU through life. It is called your life-path. Some call it 'The Way'. Each rabbit has their own path or way and rarely are two paths the same. Each individual rabbit must find its own path. If you are very lucky, you will find another rabbit that walks the same path as you and then you can walk together for awhile.'

Golden Rabbit continued. 'This morning we have been learning how easy it is to get lost and then have no idea which path to take. There are too many smells to distract and confuse you, too many directions to baffle you. Sometimes, even too many fruits to tempt you. You eventually arrived at a crossroads and could go no further because the choices confused you, and you could not tell where the truth of what you were seeking lay.'

'Arriving at a crossroads happens every day in life. Sometimes it is a big crossroads with many directions and choices. Sometimes there are only two directions. The skill is to walk the right path that leads to your destiny, Rahh. The one true path for you.'

Golden Rabbit continued. 'Life is like walking through a dense, dark forest. Sometimes we take a wrong turn and usually end up at a dead end where we cannot continue. We might find a great hole that we have actually fallen into because of our stupidity, or a foul stink that has tainted our light because we were not wise in our choice. But you were wise, Rahh. At least you could see where you were going, even though you were on the wrong path. You saw the hole and didn't fall in. You smelt the stink and didn't drink at the watering mirror, but other rabbits are not so wise. Sometimes we carry on for a long time on the wrong path until we truly realise that we are lost and confused. That is when the truly wise rabbits stop, think and try to feel the truth before taking another step.'

'We all have different paths in life. We are guided on our paths by a light within our beating fur, but you have to learn how to feel the inner light, Rahh. You have to learn how to feel the truth of where your light wishes you to go and that may be in completely the opposite direction of where you want to go.'

Rahh knew these words were important and he was paying great attention to Golden Rabbit. It was as if he could see the words falling from her mouth like a stream of golden water.

Rahh said, 'How do I find the way, Golden Rabbit?'

'The way is paved with gold, Rahh, and finding it means learning when to stop and feel the true direction. You must first learn two very important things: these will always help you find the way. They are called keys, or The Laws of the Forest Paths.'

'The first Law of the Forest is that you cannot walk the path alone all the time, for sometimes you will get lost and you will need help.'

'The second Law of the Forest is that you must learn to reach out and ask for help when you are lost or confused. This second Law is where most creatures make their errors of judgement. They continue trying to find the way by themselves, but they don't realise that they need guidance because their own light is not yet bright enough for them to see which way to go. Many rabbits waste a lot of time and energy trying to find the way, when clearly, they cannot see it.'

'When you ask for help, the great light that is within all creatures will try to give you directions through the one you ask. But there is one very important thing to learn about this. If you ask a blind rabbit for directions, then you will both fall into the hole that awaits you. But if you ask a rabbit that is full of light and wisdom, they will help you to find the way.'

Golden Rabbit went on, 'This morning, I wanted you to lead us to find good, sweet grass so that we could enjoy a good breakfast together. But I knew you could not find it in a strange woodland, and that you would get lost. Once you were lost, I could then teach you how to find your path.'

'So, here we are at this crossroads with lots of animal tracks and different smells and they are all going a different way. Many rabbits would follow another creature rather than work hard to find its own path. In that way, many rabbits and other creatures begin to rely on the direction-finding of another, and in that way, like the blind rabbit, sooner or later they will all fall into the hole because they did not work to bring their own light out of their beating fur to speak within them. Most rabbits act like sheep and follow each other, rather than standing alone and feeling for the true direction.'

'At this moment, Rahh, you are at a crossroads and you don't know which way to go. But you are a wise bunny, young and eager to learn. This morning I have given you the keys to find your way, but are you wise enough to use them, or will you continue going down a path that is not your destiny?'

'Did you listen well, Rahh?'

'Yes, Golden Rabbit,' said Rahh. 'I heard your words with my great ears and I felt them with my whiskers, and inside I could feel my light telling me that these were wise and important words, and that I should hear them carefully.'

'Golden Rabbit, I am not very clever and it seems that I have a lot to learn. Can you please help me to find the right path to take to find some more, sweet, wet grass?'

'Yes, Rahh,' replied Golden Rabbit. 'It will be my great pleasure to help you find your path. Thank you for asking me the way. That is very wise of you. It will save you much time.'

'The path through the forest is just the same as the path through life. They are identical. A crossroads is merely an opportunity to make a choice, and so we have many choices to make each day. When you arrive at a crossroads of choice you have to stop and 'feel' which way is the right way. You don't need to be clever in the head. You have to be clever in your beating fur in your chest.'

'Inside you, Rahh, is a great vessel of wisdom, but the wisdom sleeps until you open the vessel and awaken the wisdom. We call the vessel your heart, which you have heard other rabbits speak about. You know the word, but not many rabbits truly know what it is. They think it just pumps the fur up and down and goes faster when you run, and sometimes you have to rest it. But there is much truth about the heart that most rabbits have never experienced and it takes time to learn this truth. Essentially, the heart is a doorway that you can open. Behind that doorway are many other doors, each with magic and mystery behind them. Each holding a key and a map to the path that leads to your destiny.'

'When you awaken the heart, it beats to the tune of life but it also beats to the tune of the light within, which guides you through life. It lights your way. It lightens the darkness so that you can see where you are going,' said Golden Rabbit.

'True intelligence is having the courage to ask the way when you are lost. Being asleep when you are awake is staying lost. The clever rabbits are those who ask the way. How many clever rabbits do you know, Rahh?'

'I don't know any,' said Rahh.

'That is right,' said Golden Rabbit. 'As you walk through the forest of life you will meet many rabbits. They get up in the morning, go and eat the green grass and return to the burrow at night. They are the living dead. They never asked the way and each day they do the same things until they enter the long rabbit sleep. And they think that has been a great life. The only great thing about it was their emptiness because they never asked the one great question of life.'

Golden Rabbit waited to see if Rahh was still paying attention.

'What is the great question, Golden Rabbit?' asked Rahh.

'It is, 'How do I find my light?'' said Golden Rabbit.

'It is true that indeed, the path is paved with gold. But there are not many who truly wish to walk it, Rahh. However, that is a lesson for another day.'

'The light inside you is strong, Rahh, but you have not yet learned how to awaken it fully or to use it. So I will help you to find the way. Do you remember where we went yesterday?' said Golden Rabbit.

'Yes,' said Rahh. 'We went into a lovely field that was lit with the Great Light in the blue. It was warm and comfortable.'

'That's right. And where was the Great Light in the blue at the time we were in the field?'

Rahh, feeling very pleased with himself, replied, 'It was behind us. We stepped into the field and turned our backs to the Great Light in the blue.'

'And what did we follow?' asked Golden Rabbit.

'We followed the leading rabbit's foot,' said Rahh.

'That's right,' said Golden Rabbit. 'We turned to the left in the direction of the foot that rabbits always lead with, and the Great Light was behind us. So, now can you 'feel' the right path, Rahh?'

Rahh thought for a moment and said, 'I am not sure.'

Golden Rabbit asked, 'How did it feel with the Great Light behind you?'

Rahh replied immediately, 'It felt warm, lovely and safe.'

'That's correct,' said Golden Rabbit. 'So you are trying to 'feel' a feeling that is warm, lovely and safe and that feeling will show you the right path or the way you must go each time you come to a crossroad or a choice.'

Rahh jumped up and down, hopped in a circle excitedly and said, 'I think I know how to find my path. I have to get that same feeling that is warm, lovely and safe. So I must find the Great Light in the blue and position myself so I feel the same as when I was in the lovely field of grass.'

'That's right, Rahh!' said Golden Rabbit and she hopped twice to show that she was very pleased with him.

Rahh hopped to the centre of the patch of sunlight and turned his body until the warmth of the Great Light was on his back. He sat for a moment and then put out his left foot and said to Golden Rabbit, 'I think this is the way to the warm, lovely and safe field that is full of good, sweet grass. But I am confused again, Golden Rabbit.'

'What is your confusion, Rahh?'

'There is no path in this direction,' said Rahh. 'No creatures have been this way before.'

'Does this direction still feel right to you, Rahh?'

'Yes. I can still feel the warmth inside me,' said Rahh.

'Then you must make your own path, Rahh. You must be a leader, a trail-blazer walking where no other rabbits dare to walk. When you walk a new path upon the earth, others will question it. Some will call you a fool for not following the old paths or the

[30]

old ways, but others who are wise may follow your path, Rahh,' said Golden Rabbit.

'But I am afraid to walk where no other rabbits have walked,' said Rahh.

'Yes,' said Golden Rabbit. 'We are often in fear of taking a step that no other rabbit has taken. We are often in fear of making a new path. But if the fear wins, you will never learn if your heart was telling you the truth. You must overcome this fear and walk the path, totally trusting that warm feeling inside you. The more you can do this, the stronger the light will become as it beats through your fur; and the stronger the light becomes, the easier you will find your path,' said Golden Rabbit.

'But how do you make a new path, Golden Rabbit?'

'You take one simple step at a time. Today you have become a greater rabbit, Rahh, for you can feel the Great Light in the blue and also the light inside your fur and you know which direction it points you.'

'You have learned what to do when you are at a crossroads. You ask a wise rabbit for guidance.'

'You learned the Laws of the Forest paths and to ask the way. Only fools do not ask the way. But you also learned not to ask a blind rabbit for the directions, as they cannot see the way. That's a most important lesson.'

'You have heard that The Way is paved with gold, but you do not know what that means yet; and you have learned how to find your way through the forest of life, by feeling the warm, lovely and safe feelings inside.'

'All you need now, Rahh, is the courage to take the next step.'

'Let us go now and eat a proper breakfast together of the sweetest grass you ever did taste Rahh, in that field where you feel warm, lovely and safe inside.'

Golden Rabbit sat up tall and pushed out her chest. Her ears stood straight and she bristled her whiskers at Rahh, to show how much she loved him.

Rahh felt the warm feeling coming from her and it made him strong.

Golden Rabbit stamped her foot three times on the earth and said, 'Lead on, Great Rahh. Make your own path through the forest and lead us to some good, wet, sweet grass. I am getting hungry.'

Rahh pointed his whiskers before him, turned, put his head down and parted the tall grass in front of him.

Taking one step at a time, Rahh started on his own first path in life towards the true destiny of his heart.

9

The Mystery of the Blue

Rahh led Golden Rabbit back to the sunny field. Already it was mid-cycle, with the Great Light directly above them. They had spent such a long time in the wood finding the way this morning, but it didn't matter as much was spoken about and much was learned. The rabbits found a lovely spot and ate breakfast grass, as breakfast grass tasted good at any time of the day. However, the juicy wetness had gone beneath the warmth of the Great Light. No matter, they ate together and loved being with each other in this wonderful green field.

After eating, Golden Rabbit lay down and stretched her legs out behind her. When Rahh was full of the sweet grass, he too lay down next to Golden Rabbit. Nothing was said, but a few satisfied sounds were heard between them. They both dozed peacefully, not stirring until it began to get cooler.

Rahh woke up with a start and felt a little bit of fear in his tummy. Golden Rabbit sensed his fear straightaway and put her paw on his shoulder to reassure him.

'What troubles you, Rahh?' she asked.

Rahh replied. 'It is late in the cycle of light, and unsafe for rabbits to be out like this.'

'Who said it is unsafe, Rahh?'

Rahh thought for a moment and could not think of anyone who had said it was unsafe.

'I don't know,' said Rahh.

'Well, think about it, Rahh,' said Golden Rabbit. 'Think about who said to you that it is unsafe.'

Rahh thought and thought but could not think of anyone.

He said, 'I don't know! I just think that must be what is written in the Rabbit Law.'

Golden Rabbit lifted her ears lazily, as she didn't really want to get up yet. She was still enjoying the late rays of the Great Light as he dipped towards his wife, Mother Earth. However, she could see that Rahh's fear demanded a teaching to allow it to leave him, so she sat up and looked at him. Rahh sat up too and looked at Golden Rabbit.

'Look around you, Rahh, and tell me what you see,' said Golden Rabbit.

Rahh was suddenly feeling very clever because they had done this the day before and he had remembered the answers.

'I see grass and earth and sky,' said Rahh proudly.

Golden Rabbit laughed. 'Yes,' she said, 'you learned that yesterday. Well done. But do you see any danger?'

Rahh looked around him and all he could see was grass and earth and sky. As hard as he looked he could not see danger.

'No,' said Rahh. 'I cannot see any danger.'

'Do you still feel the fear in your tummy, Rahh?' asked Golden Rabbit.

'No,' replied Rahh. 'The fear has gone and I feel safe. But all my brothers and sisters will be in their burrows now because they will be in fear and think that it is unsafe as it gets cooler.'

Golden Rabbit lay down again and stretched out her long legs.

She said, 'Lie down again, Rahh; stretch out your long rabbit legs and tell me how it feels.'

Rahh lay down and stretched out his long rabbit legs, and he could still feel the warmth of the Great Light on his fur. All was still warm and safe.

Rahh said, 'I feel comfortable, warm and safe and I have no fear anymore.'

He watched as Golden Rabbit rolled on to her back and looked up into the blue.

'Do what I do,' said Golden Rabbit.

[34]

Rahh said, 'But rabbits don't lie on their backs.'

'Why not?' asked Golden Rabbit.

'Because we cannot run through the blue. We can only run on the earth and so we stay that way up all the time with our feet on the earth,' he answered.

Golden Rabbit looked with one eye at Rahh and laughed playfully with him.

'Lie on your back, Rahh, and then you will see what other rabbits do not see.'

Rahh wondered for a moment if Golden Rabbit was tricking him. His old fear of not being clever enough came back and he wanted to run into the wood and hide down a burrow.

'You can't run,' laughed Golden Rabbit, because she could feel his running fear. 'It is time for you to stop running and overcome your silly fears.'

'But my fears are real,' said Rahh.

'No they are not,' replied Golden Rabbit with a chuckle. 'You only think they are. If you look at your first fear – the fear that it is not safe at this time of day – you can't even think who told you that. Isn't that right, Rahh?'

Rahh grunted, twitched his nose and then nodded his head in agreement. He didn't quite have the courage to speak about it.

'What you did was pick up the fear from all the other rabbits, like you pick up the rain on your fur when the clouds water the earth. Once you are wet with fear from the others, you think it is your fear too. Each time one of the rabbits feels fear, it runs away and all the others run too because they feel each other's fear. It will always be the same until one rabbit stands still and truly feels if there is anything to be frightened of. All animals are affected by the thoughts and feelings of others, and they all behave the same. They run like a pack of wild, blind squirrels, because none of them has the courage to stop and feel the truth. They are all afraid to be left behind and standing alone. But most of the time, there is nothing to be afraid of.'

'You will learn how to stand alone, Rahh, and be strong.'

Golden Rabbit continued speaking.

'So every afternoon, all rabbits spend time in the dark burrow instead of in the warmth beneath the Great Light in the blue, because they think that it is unsafe. Your thought was not the truth, Rahh, but all the rabbits make it their truth because nobody ever questioned it and tested it: they were too much in fear of the truth. So rabbits live in the dark during the best time of light in their lives.'

Rahh was looking intently at Golden Rabbit. He thought that she was mad and that they were not safe and he wanted to run again.

She sensed his fear and said to him, 'Rahh, if you run from this fear that you feel now, then you will run from it for your whole life. Let the fear go and feel the truth of where you are right now.'

Rahh felt the warmth of the Great Light again and it was truly very cosy here in the grass with his full tummy, and then he relaxed a little bit and felt some of the fear leaving him.

'How does it feel now, Rahh?' asked Golden Rabbit.

'It feels better,' he said.

'Now lie on your back like me and tell me what you see.'

Rahh felt that he could try what Golden Rabbit suggested. He rolled onto his back, but overbalanced and fell on to his side again. Golden Rabbit laughed at his efforts to be the 'wrong' way up.

Rahh laughed too and tried again. This time he made it. He was balancing on his back on the earth looking into the blue.

'What do you see now, Rahh?' asked Golden Rabbit.

Rahh, feeling clever again, replied, 'I can see the blue, Golden Rabbit, but this time it is upside down and my feet are in it.'

Golden Rabbit laughed again. 'Is the blue upside down, or are you upside down, Rahh?' she asked.

Rahh said, 'Well I'm not sure now. Perhaps the blue can't be upside down, so it must be me that is upside down.'

[36]

'Perhaps you are just seeing things differently, and neither is upside down. They are just different because you are looking at life differently.'

Well, that was confusing for a rabbit, as they always look at things the same way, like most other animals; but Rahh was learning a lot of lessons this past couple of days and began to realise that each time Golden Rabbit showed him something new, his heart and mind expanded and he could see differently.

Golden Rabbit asked Rahh another question.

'Rahh,' she said. 'When you run as a rabbit runs across the grass and into the wood, do you run in a straight line?'

Rahh knew the answer to this immediately.

'Of course not,' he said. 'We have to run around fence posts, trees, brambles and a hundred different things, so it is impossible to run in a straight line because of all the obstacles.'

'Now look into the blue again,' she said, 'and tell me what you see.'

Rahh replied immediately. 'I still see just the blue and my feet.'

'Very well,' said Golden Rabbit. 'Tell me what you can't see in the blue.'

Rahh thought for a while about this tricky question. How could he see things that he couldn't see? Eventually he had to give up, and said, 'I can't see those things you are asking me to see Golden Rabbit, because they are not there.' He laughed.

'If that is the truth, Rahh, shall I tell you what you can't see?'

'Oh yes please, Golden Rabbit,' laughed Rahh, 'because I am upside down and going dizzy looking for these invisible things that don't exist in the empty blue above my feet.'

Golden Rabbit laughed too. Rahh was definitely developing his sense of humour.

'When you run from the field to the woods, Rahh, you said that you have to run around all kinds of obstacles. Well, when a rabbit runs through the blue, there are no obstacles. It is a clear path of emptiness.'

'So, when you are upside down with your feet in the blue, you can run through the blue and get where you are going very quickly because there are no difficult things to avoid.'

'But how can a rabbit run through the blue?' puzzled Rahh.

'We call running through the blue '*HesiMed*' and it gets you to where you need to be very quickly.'

'*HesiMed*,' repeated Rahh with his eyes wide open, trying to see if there was an obstacle to this thinking.

'Yes,' said Golden Rabbit. 'Some call it 'Stopalot', and some of the two-leggeds call it 'blue sky thinking'.'

'Well, what is it?' asked Rahh.

'Here is the most important question of the day. What can you see in the blue, Rahh?' Golden Rabbit said.

Rahh fell off his back onto his side, jumped up and ran round in a circle.

'Golden Rabbit,' he exclaimed with exasperation in his voice. 'I can't see anything in the blue because there is nothing in it.' He put his head onto the ground and his paws over his ears. He thought his head was going to explode.

Golden Rabbit laughed at his antics.

'You are so funny, Rahh – but I must say, well done! That is correct. There is nothing in the blue. It is empty. That is the point you need to see, Rahh.'

Rahh continued to keep his ears under his paws, but he could still hear Golden Rabbit's words.

'Now listen carefully, Rahh. When you make a rabbit empty, like the blue, then you can find all the answers you need.'

'*HesiMed* means to *Hesitate and Meditate*. Or in the case of 'Stopalot', when you come to a problem in life, you stop and stay stopped until you become empty like the blue. We remove all the obstacles so that we can see where we want to go. Then we turn over, get on our feet again and just go there, avoiding all obstacles. We are able to do this because we stop thinking like rabbits full of fear, and we open our hearts to the blue. And

[38]

the Great Light in the blue helps to show us the way. Ordinary rabbits stink of think, but rabbits that feel the truth of the way eventually *become.*'

This was a lot of new information for Rahh to take in. His little bunny head was suddenly full up and he felt the weight of all this stinky thinky stuff in his tummy. He was so surprised that he was full up that he jumped up in the air as if in fright and ran round in another circle.

Golden Rabbit was still lying serenely on her back gazing into the blue, chuckling to herself. She said, 'Did you feel your old fear again, then, Rahh?'

Rahh was embarrassed. 'Yes,' he said. 'It was very strange. It was as if my body was taken over by the fear and it jumped up all by itself and ran round in a circle.'

'Yes,' said Golden Rabbit. 'That is how strong fear is when it is in your body. It can make you do things against your will. It takes your body over and makes you run. But if you practise 'Stopalot', letting go of the fear and doing things in a different way, the fear loses its power over you and leaves your body. Then you become free.'

Golden Rabbit continued.

'When there are too many things to do or think about, just stop, roll onto your back and gaze into the blue where there are no obstacles. Just look into the blue and listen to how your thoughts are out of control. Look into the nothingness and allow your thoughts to melt away. Allow them to float up into the blue.'

'The blue is clear, it has no obstacles, so it brings clarity to your mind and body. When you have clarity, you can solve many difficult things, like when is the best time to eat breakfast grass,' laughed Golden Rabbit. 'Now that is an important thing to know, as the breakfast grass will nurture you and help you to grow, Rahh.'

Golden Rabbit laughed at her own joke and Rahh laughed too, then he said, 'What do you become free from, Golden Rabbit?'

'You become free of all the thoughts and fears of other rabbits; and you become very strong in your heart. You will see the other rabbits running around, being driven by their fears and following all the other fear-filled rabbits. But you will stand alone, on your own, standing in your own power because you learned to see things differently. You learned to see the truth by becoming still and empty, like the blue.'

'All the other rabbits will be running around in the same old way for the whole of their lives, but your life will constantly change as you keep letting go of the fears that make you a rabbit,' said Golden Rabbit.

Rahh could see that Golden Rabbit was very serious and her words were now coming from a very deep place inside her. He knew that these were important words and he should take them into himself deeply.

'Golden Rabbit, may I ask another question please?'

'Yes, of course, Rahh.'

'If I stop being a rabbit, then what will I become?'

'You will just become, Rahh. You will just become.'

'As the Great Light passes through many, many cycles, Rahh, you will eventually become; and then you will know what I mean.'

10

Meeting the Girabbits

It had been a very long day. Rahh thought that this had been the longest day of his life, because normally he would have been in the earth for most of it; but today he had been out of the burrow from the time when the Great Light rose into the blue, and now it was dropping so low that it had almost disappeared behind the hills.

'I think it is time for us to go to the burrow,' said Golden Rabbit. 'It is time for us to rest and recover because tomorrow we have another journey to go on.'

Golden Rabbit led the way and Rahh followed behind her. They entered the wood and hopped to Rahh's new burrow.

'Shall we meet in the morning again, Rahh?' asked Golden Rabbit.

'Oh yes please,' replied Rahh.

'Then I will be here when you are ready to awaken. Rest well little bunny, and dream the sweetest dreams in all the woodland.'

'Thank you Golden Rabbit, and you too, I wish you some lovely dreams,' said Rahh.

Rahh put his ears back and popped down into mother earth and Golden Rabbit went her own way.

Rahh's new burrow was very deep. In fact, it seemed deeper than the night before. This was only his second night in the new burrow but it felt very homely and comfortable. There was lovely bedding of fresh, sweet-smelling straw and even a few dandelion leaves, as if they had been placed there in case he woke up hungry in the night, and there was soft dry grass on the straw, too, to make the bed more luxurious. Rahh sniffed the air and flicked his whiskers up and down to sense the space around him. Everything was clean and dry with a sweet smell. He turned around three times and then settled down on his lovely bed. He pulled the straw up under his chin like a little pillow and suddenly felt quite tired, the smell of camomile flowers drifted into his nose, as his eyes closed and his breathing relaxed. He was alone, but he wasn't lonely. He felt warm and loved and knew that he was safe.

Rahh soon drifted into a deep sleep, but it was a busy sleep because he began to dream almost immediately. In the dream he bounced out of the burrow into a bright sunny morning and began his journey through the wood.

All around were very tall rabbits. They were huge. They were ten times the size of Rahh with very tall, long necks: they looked more like giraffes than rabbits! He thought these must be the Girabbits of legend, the ones who ate fruit from the tallest trees and kept their heads above the clouds.

The Girabbits all had their heads so far into the blue that Rahh couldn't even see them. All he could really see were their long necks, which disappeared above into the morning mists. Of course, none of the Girabbits could see Rahh down below either, and he had to keep dodging their huge feet so that they didn't tread on him accidentally. He thought to himself that he'd better shout out and let them know he was there.

'Hello up there,' he shouted, but they didn't hear him. Again he shouted as loud as he could, 'Hey. Hey you up there.' Some of them stopped talking and twitched their whiskers and looked around at each other with a questioning look of, 'Did you hear something?' Then one of them lowered his head beneath the mist, looked down and saw tiny Rahh at his feet.

'Ah look, ladies and gentlemen, down below in the moss and the mirk. It is one of those stinky thinky rabbits that run around like fools, never really knowing what is going on but always fearing the worst.'

Ho, ho, ho, they all laughed mockingly.

Suddenly a whole tribe of Girabbits' giant heads peered through the misty layers at Rahh below them. Rahh felt very small and somewhat intimidated, but he knew that he was actually very brave. He shouted back at them, 'I am not a stinky thinky rabbit. I am Rahh and one day you will know me.'

The tall Girabbits raised their heads above the mist with an air of aloofness. They looked at each other questioningly, then bent down again to look at Rahh. They were impressed that this little rabbit had spoken up for himself. Clearly he had something about him that the other stinky thinky rabbits did not, as they usually ran away when a Girabbit looked at them. Once they had had a good look at Rahh, they raised their heads again. Rahh thought it was very funny to see all these necks disappearing into the mist with no heads on top of them.

One Girabbit bent his head down again to look more closely at Rahh, and then he spoke.

'You say your name is Rahh?'

'Yes, I am Rahhhhhhh.' The sound of his name came out like a lion's roar and he bared his teeth in a mock growl. 'And I am no ordinary rabbit. I am special.'

Rahh was quite surprised by the lion's growl that came out of him and his whiskers were still shaking from the sound.

'Welcome then, special rabbit Rahhhhhh,' said the Girabbit with a little mockery in his voice. He raised his head into the clouds again and encouraged them all to welcome him. There was a great sound of mmm's and ahhh's as they agreed with the speaker that a welcome was in order, but without actually saying it.

The speaker lowered his head again and spoke.

'And how are you special, Rahhhhhh? Would you like to share that with us?' said the Girabbit. Heads appeared below the mist again, nodding in agreement that they would like to know the answer to this question. How was this great and marvellous new rabbit special?

Rahh felt strong inside, but also a little confused, as he did not

[43]

know how he was special; he just had a feeling that he was but could not explain it.

He puffed out his little furry chest and said with confidence, 'I am special because *I know* that I am.'

The Girabbits lifted their heads again. Rahh heard a lot of whiskers twitching accompanied by all manner of mumbling sounds. Soon enough, the Girabbits all went quiet and looked down at Rahh again.

Presently, the head of the speaker came down lower and said. 'We would like to see your pieces of paper?'

'What pieces of paper?' asked Rahh.

'The pieces of paper with the gold seal to say how special and important you are,' replied the Girabbit.

'I have no pieces of paper,' said Rahh. 'Why would I need pieces of paper?'

The speaking Girabbit grunted and lifted his head to the others. 'It is as we thought, the stinky thinky rabbit has no paper to say how important he is.'

Hurrumph, Hmmm, Grrrr and other such noises of disapproval were heard by Rahh as the heads went back into the mist. Then the speaker appeared again, looking sternly at Rahh.

'Hmmm, small rabbit,' said the speaker. 'We are very busy. We have important matters to discuss. We have airs and graces to maintain and we must keep our heads high so that we can see more clearly than those with their noses in the earth. We cannot put our heads down here all day to listen to your story of how special you think you are, but indeed you must be special to have found yourself amongst us. One day perhaps you will grow in stature with pieces of paper to say how important you are. When you bring us your paper, of course, we will recognise you.'

'For now, you must pass along and we will not delay you any longer on your important journey. Perhaps when you can speak about how special you are, you will pass this way again and let us know, so that we are fully informed.'

[44]

Rahh looked at them, feeling relieved that he was not going to be trampled by their big feet or even interrogated any further.

'Thank you for your kindness,' he said politely.

Heads still in the mist, all the Girabbits except the speaker stood back a little so that Rahh could pass.

The speaker asked, 'Which way are you going?'

Rahh pointed towards a faint golden glow deep in the wood, and said, 'I feel like that is my way, towards the light. That is my destination, or my destiny, or both.'

Rahh thanked them and walked through the corridor made by their legs and towards the golden glow in the distance.

The Knowledge Quest

Rahh awoke very refreshed and stepped out of his burrow into a bright morning. He realised that he was up later than usual because the Great Light in the blue was already blazing and bathing the earth with its warmth. Mist was rising from the grass and the leaves swayed in a gentle breeze around him. Golden Rabbit was not here yet and so Rahh sniffed about the earth and settled to nibble some small, juicy leaves whilst he waited for her to arrive.

A few moments later he became aware of a gentle golden glow moving silently through the woodland. He knew that this was Golden Rabbit, but the glow was so bright today, even beneath the brightness of the Great Light in the blue; it seemed much brighter than he remembered yesterday.

Golden Rabbit stepped into the little glade where Rahh's burrow lay.

'Good morning, Rahh,' she said, taking a deep breath of air.

'Good morning, Golden Rabbit,' replied Rahh enthusiastically, as he looked at how bright she was shining. In fact, he could feel her light shining very deeply inside of him as if a great warmth radiated from her.

'How are you this fine morning?' she asked.

'I am very furry, thank you,' answered Rahh, which was a rabbit way of saying that he felt extremely good.

'Was your burrow cosy and did you sleep well?'

'Oh yes, thank you, very well indeed,' Rahh replied.

'I was so warm and comfortable,' then he remembered his dream, and continued, 'and I had a very funny dream about very tall rabbits, as tall as giraffes, with long necks and their heads so high that they were in the clouds. I call them Girabbits because of their long necks.'

'Ah yes,' said Golden Rabbit, nodding knowingly.

'Do you know them?' asked Rahh, surprised.

'Oh yes,' said Golden Rabbit, nodding knowingly again. 'They are the animals who inhabit a different part of the wood. They have become lost to themselves on the knowledge-quest and now their heads have become stuck above the clouds, where they can't see the truth of anything any longer,' said Golden Rabbit.

'What is the knowledge-quest?' asked Rahh.

'It is like a fever, where the animal allows their head to become stronger than their heart. When that happens they become out of balance with life,' replied Golden Rabbit.

'In your head, Rahh, is your brain. It is your thinking part that helps you to make decisions. It is a great power source, like the Great Light in the blue. But if you don't learn how to switch it off and allow it to rest, then it can get out of balance and run away with your life. It becomes an animal itself, living inside you. It becomes a monster, so hungry for knowledge that it continues to seek, seek, seek to feed, feed, feed,' said Golden Rabbit.

'The brain puts all this knowledge into the mind, which becomes like a library of knowledge or knowing things – often useless things of little importance.'

'Some animals think that if they have a lot of knowledge in the mind-library, they are clever; but in reality, those who can still the brain and empty the mind are indeed the clever ones,' Golden Rabbit went on.

'Is the mind in the head, too?' asked Rahh.

'No, Rahh. The mind is everywhere, all around you and out beyond the blue. Sometimes when we put things in the mind to remember for later, we can't find where we put them because it is so big,' chuckled Golden Rabbit.

Rahh was very interested in trying to find out how to put things in his mind, and listened intently to Golden Rabbit.

'The brain seeks the food, which is called knowledge, and the mind stores it so that the animal can remember the knowledge and bring it back later. This is called re-calling the knowledge. As the mind stores more things, it becomes stronger too and can also become an animal in its own right, with a life-force.'

'The more things the mind knows, the more intelligent the animal thinks it is!' she continued, by now almost falling over laughing. She put her nose on the ground between her paws and laughed till her ears flopped forward. Rahh laughed too, even though he was not yet sure what a brain, mind and knowledge were.

'Can you imagine, Rahh, the mind being like a burrow, and in that burrow you keep digging more rooms where you can store things. If you filled all the rooms with nuts from the forest, would that make you intelligent or foolish?'

Rahh thought for a moment and said, 'Well, I think, Golden Rabbit, that you would have food for many, many cycles of the Great Light, so would that not be intelligent and clever?'

'Of course not Rahh, it would show that you were stupid,' laughed Golden Rabbit.

'Oh,' said Rahh, suddenly feeling a little lost for an answer and looking at Golden Rabbit for an explanation.

'Well,' said Golden Rabbit. 'It would show that you had no trust in the mother to bring you food each day. You would have used your valuable time to do all this work to fill your life with things that you don't need. You will have done all that work and spent all that time of your life to fill up your space so that there was nothing left. I don't think that is very intelligent. Of course, we need to know a few things so that life runs as smoothly as it can, but to cram a woodland full of nuts into your living space would be the act of a mad rabbit, and that's why rabbits don't do that in general. But there are always some who like to show

[48]

the world that they have more nuts than others,' laughed Golden Rabbit. 'It is called bravado. Puffing out your chest to show the world how big you are, and at the same time how foolish,' said Golden Rabbit, shaking her head in dismay.

Golden Rabbit stopped laughing, composed herself and sat up again. Rahh looked deeply into her eyes, eager to hear more of the story.

'Really, Rahh, it is not very funny, even though I laugh. It is a cruel thing to do, but sometimes you see things in life that are so bizarre and ridiculous that you cannot help but laugh. But it is a laugh that is full of pain for those who cannot see and are blind in the heart.'

'Intelligence is not how much knowledge you have, but who you are in your heart, Rahh. Intelligence is what your heart brings into the world, not what your head takes out of it,' she said.

'Eventually, the mind can take over the animal and its neck becomes so long that its head goes through the clouds and it loses sight of the meaning of its own life. At this point the animal becomes a Mirror Head. Once its head rises above the clouds it can only look down on other animals because they are not as full up with knowledge. The Mirror Head then only sees other animals, whose heads are above the clouds too, with the same disease of mind-fever. When they look at each other, all they see is a mirror-like reflection of what they have become,' said Golden Rabbit.

'The problem often starts when the animal is still a pup or a kitten, very young. The parents of the animal constantly tell it that it must work very hard and fill itself with knowledge. In this game, when you allow your mind to eat a lot of knowledge, then the leaders of the knowledge-game give you pieces of paper that tell you how many things you know, and how clever you are.'

'The parents often tell the pup what it is going to do and be in its life. They drive even more knowledge into it. They never stop to feel the truth of the pup carefully, with love, or to see what gifts of life it has been given to bring into the world. The gifts of life are given by the Great Light that illuminates the heart of all beings. The gifts live in the heart until someone helps to bring them out,' Golden Rabbit explained.

'With all the pressure to learn things and gather pieces of paper, the animal loses its way in life. It quite often forgets to live a life of joy and to seek the truth of the gifts inside itself. It only has a focus on gathering pieces of paper and walking a path with others of the same kind. Most of the animals in this game live a life of fear. They fear that they will not get enough pieces of paper and that others in the game will laugh at them. They live in fear of ridicule and being told that they are not good enough. As they get older, the fear grows, because they did not develop the truth of who they are in their core; in their centre; in their heart.'

'They become the victims in their chosen game of life, only being able to prosper and grow if those at the head of the game allow them to have pieces of paper.'

'In this game, you are not seen for the Great Light that shines within you, instead you are judged by those with the most pieces of paper and how much of your mind-burrow is full of nuts,' said Golden Rabbit, suddenly chuckling again and shaking her head in disbelief.

'In this chosen life, the body often becomes filled with a fear that it hasn't eaten enough knowledge. The fear of failing to get paper drives the animal on until quite often, at a certain point, the life breaks down and everything stops, except for the tears, which flow and flow and flow.

'Sometimes, when the animal has many, many pieces of paper, it begins to see itself as supremely important. At that point, its head goes right out into the blue where it can never reconnect with its own treasure within again. It is very sad to see such an animal, as it lives in a world of illusion.'

Golden Rabbit stopped speaking and just gazed at Rahh. She seemed suddenly empty.

Rahh felt it was important not to say anything, and so he sat and watched her. He could feel her sadness for the Girabbits and a tear was on her cheek. She bowed her head to nibble a few leaves and Rahh did the same.

It seemed that the speaking had finished for now, but Rahh could feel the pain in Golden Rabbit's heart for all those who were lost to paper and could not find the true nature of the light they had brought into the world we all share.

12

The Mirror Heads

'Did the tall rabbits notice you, Rahh?'

'Well, it was only a dream,' said Rahh.

Golden Rabbit looked carefully at Rahh and then spoke.

'Many important messages come to you during the dark-time Rahh, but it takes wisdom and practice to understand them. This was not just a dream, it was the light within giving you an important message. So, did the tall ones notice you?'

Rahh replied. 'Not at first, I had to shout up to them twice as I was afraid that they would trample me underfoot. One of them bent his long neck down and looked at me. He then spoke to the others, calling me a 'stinky thinky rabbit'. That gave me a pain inside.'

'Yes,' said Golden Rabbit, 'that is because they see you as below them in all things, including your physical stature; but the meek and pure in heart will find the way, Rahh, not those with their heads in the clouds.'

Rahh continued, 'But I then felt strong inside and I told them that I was not a stinky thinky rabbit. I told them I was Rahhhhhh and my voice was like a lion roaring. It quite made me jump and my whiskers shook, and I told them I was special, too.'

'In what way did you tell them you were special, Rahh?' asked Golden Rabbit.

'Well, they asked me how I was special, but I didn't know. I just felt that I was,' said Rahh.

'It is very good that you could feel that, Rahh,' said Golden Rabbit. 'What happened next?'

'The Girabbits told me they were busy discussing important

matters. They said that perhaps one day I would have pieces of paper to say how important I am and then they would recognise me. Then they stepped aside and let me pass,' said Rahh.

'You are my student and I will teach you,' said Golden Rabbit.

Being called a student made Rahh feel very important inside. His whiskers bristled upwards and his eyes lit up with joy.

Golden Rabbit continued.

'All animals have two great things that will grow if you nurture them. The first is the heart and the second is the mind. The heart is the most important of these. It is in your centre. It connects you between Heaven and Earth, and connects you to the truth of everything when you open it.'

'The mind seems like it is in your head, but really it is everywhere. The mind thinks it is very clever and powerful, but the trouble is, the mind can think as much as it likes but it will never be as clever as the heart. Ever, ever, ever!' said Golden Rabbit.

Rahh remained transfixed on Golden Rabbit's words. He knew they were important, but his mind was getting in the way of trying to understand them. Golden Rabbit could see that Rahh was looking confused, as rabbits often can be.

'Do you have a question about the mind and the heart, Rahh?' asked Golden Rabbit.

'Um…These words seem very big, Golden Rabbit, and I am just a small rabbit; what you say seems too big for me to understand. You already told me not to fill my mind-burrow with nuts, and now you tell me that it is important, and probably clever to grow the mind, so I am confused,' said Rahh.

'That is exactly my point, Rahh. Your lesson is not about understanding big or small things with your mind. Your lesson is to 'feel' the truth of the words with your heart.'

Of course, this complicated philosophy was equally difficult for a small bunny like Rahh to grasp, when most of the time he was more concerned with the first green blades of breakfast grass to pass his lips.

[53]

Golden Rabbit continued.

'When the mind becomes detached from the heart, it can only go upwards into the blue, seeking ever higher understanding. For every millimetre the mind reaches upwards, the neck grows and the animal's mind becomes more distant from its own heart. Eventually the animal has no true feelings because the mind takes over their lives and they become dead in the heart.'

'But if you take care to allow the mind to grow with emptiness, it will be filled with love and compassion,' said Golden Rabbit.

'So, Rahh, you didn't just have a dream. You had an encounter with the Mirror Heads. They are the ones who really stink of think because they think too much. They lose their minds chasing pieces of paper that tell them how clever and important they are. The more pieces of paper they gather, the more they look down on the animals that don't have paper. Some of them become so infected with thinking that they make a lot of important-sounding noises and like to be in charge of other animals, telling them what they can and can't do.'

'I forgot why they are called the Mirror Heads,' said Rahh.

'They are called Mirror Heads because they seek to see a reflection of their self-importance through the eyes of those who wish to be them.'

'Now, Rahh, before we continue, I will tell you a secret. I saw your dream when you were dreaming it.'

Rahh suddenly sat up tall. 'How can you see my dream?' he asked, truly surprised.

'There is a Great Light, of which I have spoken briefly. You will learn more of it soon. This Great Light is the teacher of all things that are important. It lights the way of life and it shows us what we need to see in order to find our path. When this Great Light shines brightly within you, it becomes your teacher,' said Golden Rabbit.

'Like you are my teacher now, Golden Rabbit?' asked Rahh.

'Yes. As I am your teacher now, so the Light will become your teacher when it has woken up within you.'

Golden Rabbit continued.

'As I was lying in my burrow this morning, this inner light showed me that it was teaching you through a dream and I was allowed to see it too.'

'So you already know my dream, then, Golden Rabbit,' said Rahh with eyes wide open in surprise.

'Yes, that's right Rahh.'

'Then we do not need to discuss it, because you already know it,' he replied.

'That is right too, but in order for me to teach you, we must re-live your dream and I will explain certain meanings to you. In that way you will learn how to find your way through life,' explained Golden Rabbit.

'Oh, I see,' said Rahh. 'Then please continue.'

Rahh sat back with his paws together in front of him and continued to look intently into Golden Rabbit's eyes. He thought to himself, 'I am a good student, sitting upright and paying attention. I will bristle my whiskers up too.' He was quite proud of himself, learning so much this early in the morning, even if he was still confused.

Golden Rabbit bowed her head a little to him and she bristled up her whiskers too, to show that he was important to her. Then she continued.

'Your heart spoke to them, Rahh. You roared your name in a growl and they heard it speak. The light in your heart gave you the courage of the lion so that you would not be afraid of what they thought of you. Already, even before they knew you, they judged you. They called you a stinky thinky rabbit. But your heart is growing strong and you roared your name into the clouds where their heads live. You are a great and courageous rabbit, Rahh.'

'Of course, your roar made them tremble inside, even though

they did not show it, and they could not get rid of you quickly enough. They opened a way for you to pass, but not before letting you know that you are nothing until you have pieces of paper to say how special you are. But I do not think that you will become a chaser of paper, Rahh. I do not think that you will abandon your heart and your life-mission,' smiled Golden Rabbit.

'There are many paths through the forest, Rahh, but there is only one path that is meant for each of us. It is most important that we find that path, otherwise we can become lost and empty inside and waste a whole life chasing meaningless things. Or indeed, ending up with paper that means nothing compared to the one thing that matters most and is yearned for least.'

'What is that?' asked Rahh.

'You will understand in due course,' replied Golden Rabbit.

'And in what way am I special?' asked Rahh.

'That too, little bunny, you will know in due course. Indeed, the Mirror Heads will eventually know your name, and you will not have a single piece of paper to show who you are. Many, many animals will know you by your sign.'

'And what is my sign,' Rahh enquired.

'Your sign is what spoke to the Mirror Heads, Rahh. It is your courage and what lies behind your courage, and you will find that soon enough. Now, one final word on this matter, Rahh,' said Golden Rabbit. 'Knowledge is food for the mind, and it can be a wonderful thing to have knowledge. As the mind grows we can nurture it and learn many things. Some animals become supremely intelligent and do great things for the mother earth and all animals that dwell upon her, but there is a great big 'but' that goes with this.'

'What is the 'but', Golden Rabbit?' asked Rahh.

'The 'but' is called balance. Everything in life and in our world is held in a fine balance. Every thought and deed must have balance. Every natural thing is held in balance. The Great Light in the blue goes round and round because it is in balance, and so all animals must learn to find this balance in their own lives.'

'A powerful mind can be a greedy mind, never having enough of what it seeks until it breaks. A powerful belly can fill itself too much and then pain comes into the animal. So all things must find the other side of themselves, which then creates the balance. We all have one great thing within us that will show us where the balance lies, if we seek it.'

'It is the intelligent and developed heart that beats and bounces inside your fur, Rahh. It is the living pump that drives your living insides, that allows you to experience all the wonders of the outsides. This heart is the truth of who you are and it holds the answers to everything beneath the Great Light in the blue. Yet there are no pieces of paper that you can obtain to say that you have been to the very centre of your heart and returned with the knowledge and wisdom of the truth of who you really are.'

'This is the greatest journey any animal can make, the journey to the centre of your being, to the centre of your heart. That is where the true and most valuable treasure lies and there is no paper that can tell you how to find it.'

'How do we find the way then, Golden Rabbit?'

'We find it by seeking to stand in the light of one who has found the way and been to the centre where the treasure lies, Rahh,' said Golden Rabbit.

'Any animal who has touched the gold at the centre, has but one mission in life, and that is to light the way for others that seek to find this same treasure.'

'It is the meek and gentle ones who have opened that inner door who will ultimately receive the greatest gifts in life; yet the Mirror Heads, with all their knowledge and pieces of paper, will never understand where you have been and what you have found. More than that, they will never understand the value

[57]

of it because you do not have a piece of paper to impress them.'

'It is within the heart that true intelligence lies; and it is within the mind that knowledge lies.'

'With balance, even the Mirror Heads and all paper-chasers can awaken and seek that inner path, and then their knowledge will have meaning and their lives will not have been wasted.'

'One day, Rahh, you may be the one whom the Mirror Heads seek out, so that you can teach them about true intelligence and finding their way back from the clouds into a life full of meaning, purpose and success.'

Even though Rahh was paying great attention to Golden Rabbit's words, he was very confused by this last statement. However, he soon brushed it off with thoughts of nibbling some sweet breakfast grass.

Secretly, he thought that surely, that was the most important thing for a rabbit at this time of the morning?

And such is the mystery of wisdom, that he was probably right.

13

A Light Breakfast

'Now young rabbit, I think it is time for some breakfast,' said Golden Rabbit. 'Already the blue is brightening and the mist rising, leaving the dew upon the green blades. It is time for you to eat a Light breakfast, Rahh.'

'A *light* breakfast?!' replied Rahh, with some alarm in his voice. 'But I want to eat breakfast until lunchtime, because I am very hungry after having to fight my way past the Mirror Heads all night and then being a student. I feel a bit like I need a Lion's breakfast.'

'Ahh,' said Golden Rabbit laughing. 'You misunderstand me Rahh. Did you notice anything unusual or different this morning when I arrived at your burrow?'

Rahh thought for a moment and then replied.

'Er, yes, well it was as if you were glowing like the Great Light in the blue. A great light was all around you.'

'Yes,' replied Golden Rabbit, pushing out her chest and smiling broadly at Rahh. 'I ate a Light breakfast.'

Rahh looked confused and repeated the words questioningly. 'Light breakfast? Do you mean that if you don't eat very much, you glow like the Great Light in the blue?'

Golden Rabbit laughed again, because she liked to tease Rahh as a way of helping him to learn to see things differently.

'No Rahh, I actually ate quite a lot for my breakfast, but what I ate was Light. Now I glow like a great Golden Rabbit,' and she pushed out her chest again to show how full of light she was.

'Oh,' said Rahh, with confusion all over his face and his whiskers flopping about helplessly, not really knowing what to say next.

Golden Rabbit continued. 'Today, Rahh, I will teach you one of the great lessons of all animals; not many know it. This is what will awaken the thing that is special within you – but until you look for it, find it, embrace it and love it, then you are nothing more than a rabbit.'

Rahh's whiskers sprang up again questioningly and Golden Rabbit went on.

'It is most important to understand, Rahh that each rabbit is full of the potential to become a great Golden Rabbit who shines like the Great Light in the blue. Now let us go to the Field of Wonders and eat a Light breakfast,' she said, and gave a joyful hop into the air.

'Field of Wonders? What is that?!' Rahh put his paws over his ears and felt that he could not take in any more of this new world. It was like a really difficult dream that he could not wake up from.

'It is the place where Mother and Father show us the jewels that are ours for the taking,' replied Golden Rabbit with her eyes wide open and chuckling at Rahh's exasperation.

'Golden Rabbit,' cried Rahh. 'I can't take any more surprises. I have had a night with the Mirror Heads, a roaring lion in my whiskers, the knowledge-quest, the mind-fever, the paper-chasers and now I have to eat a breakfast of Light in the Field of Wonders whilst looking for the jewels my mother and father are bringing to me … Oh Golden Rabbit, I am just a rabbit with fur in my ears. I am very small and all these new things are too much to carry!'

'Yes, you are,' replied Golden Rabbit. 'But soon you will be full of light and then you will be Becoming.'

'Oh no. Not Becoming again.'

'Yes,' Golden Rabbit replied, smiling. 'You are becoming your unique and special self, Rahh. Now follow me to the Field of Wonders and there at least your tummy will be comfortable, even if the rest of you is not.'

Golden Rabbit whistled a happy tune through her whiskers as she hopped out of the glade and into the wood. She looked over her shoulder to make sure that Rahh was following.

Rahh felt that it was a good idea not to think about anything any longer, as his confusion was so intense that he thought he might collapse. Also, he considered that it would be better not to be left behind – so he quickly hopped after Golden Rabbit.

14

Field of Wonders

As the rabbits approached the edge of the wood, they could see that the mist was still rising across the green fields, but there remained drops of clear dew on the grass. Rabbits like the grass to be a little wet in the morning, since they drink the water as they nibble the grass.

'You have to be early for a Light breakfast,' said Golden Rabbit.

'Why is that?' asked Rahh.

'It is because there is only a certain time that you can harvest the wealth that is given to us by Mother and Father.'

'Mother and father?' thought Rahh. 'I have not seen my mother and father for a long time now,' or so it seemed.

'Is it *my* mother and father,' asked Rahh, 'are they here?'

'Yes, they are here. You are born of them, they created you and brought the great whiskers of light into you that guide your life. Every step you take on the earth is with your Mother and Father. You are never separated from them, ever.'

Rahh looked through the fence into the Field of Wonders, thinking that this looked like a pretty ordinary field to him; he could not see any dreams anywhere. More than that, he couldn't see his mother or father either. He was a bit fed up with all the mystery of this new life that he had suddenly found himself in. For a moment, he longed to be with his brothers and sisters in the burrow again, to be somewhere familiar, somewhere he knew.

Golden Rabbit looked at him and could feel his sudden confusion and loneliness; his sense of having lost the life he knew, and a little bit of fear about this new unknown world.

What he needed was some rabbit comfort – some juicy grass in his tummy.

'Rahh,' she said. 'Step into the field with me and eat some grass, then rest a while under the Great Light in the blue. You are too exhausted this morning from all this learning. Eat, rest and then you will find that your light wakes up a little and you will be curious to learn more.'

Golden Rabbit led the way into the field and hopped through the hummocks to a patch of nice, moist, green grass. She lay down on her belly, as she was already full of light. She brushed the ground with her whiskers in front of Rahh, which was a rabbit invitation to browse the sweetest grass in front of her.

Rahh was a little downcast with all those feelings going around inside him, but he hopped closer to Golden Rabbit and began to run his whiskers over the grass and nibble. Even the first taste of moisture on his tongue lifted his spirits and he nuzzled the ground in thanks, lifting the green blades into his mouth and onto his tongue. He looked up into Golden Rabbit's loving eyes and felt the softness of her heart touching his life.

15

The Truth of Dreams

Rahh ate heartily, he was so hungry. It seemed like a week since he had eaten anything that filled him with green juice. Golden Rabbit lay contented, drifting, as if in a daydream beneath the warmth of the Great Light in the blue. As she drifted in and out, she kept her eye on Rahh. She watched him very closely, for he was special and he had been sent to her as a great gift. It was always a great gift to be able to help another being find the way.

Rahh's belly filled up nicely and he made little sounds of contentment. He stretched his neck upwards to the blue and then lay on his belly, full and happy. All his confusion and loneliness had melted away. It is amazing what a full belly can do for a rabbit.

'Is that better, Rahh?'

'Ooooh, Golden Rabbit, I was so hungry. I don't think I was ever that hungry in my whole life,' he replied.

He brushed his whiskers with his furry paws and put his nose down in the grass, which was a rabbit sign of deep happiness.

'Was the grass different today?' asked Golden Rabbit.

'No, I think it was just a very nice grass, but not much different from the grass that I am used to,' answered Rahh.

'Is that so, young Rahh! And I thought that you were feeling special today! You also said you knew that you were special, too, with that roaring lion shaking your whiskers this morning. Do you recall, when you told the Mirror Heads that you were special?' asked Golden Rabbit.

'That roaring was only in the dream, Golden Rabbit.'

'Oh, so you think the lion inside you was only in the dream, do you Rahh?'

'Yes. Of course, I only felt it in the dream.'

'So, was your dream inside you then, Rahh?'

'Erm ... Yes, my dream was inside me.'

'And was the roaring lion inside your dream?' she went on.

'Yes ... yes it was,' the little rabbit replied.

'So, if the roaring lion was in your dream, and your dream was inside you, then the roaring lion is inside you too, then, Rahh – is it not?' chuckled Golden Rabbit.

'Oh no,' thought Rahh. 'Here we go again with this mad world that is turning my own world upside-down with mystery.'

'How can I have a real roaring lion inside me? But perhaps it is so,' he thought. 'Anything might be possible with Golden Rabbit.'

'Oh, yes, I see that I have to admit that you are right, Golden Rabbit,' said Rahh. 'Yeees, the roaring lion must be inside me.'

Golden Rabbit laughed and then Rahh laughed too.

Golden Rabbit rolled on to her back and gazed into the blue. Her whiskers were twitching in contentment that Rahh had learned something new about dreams and how things are sometimes inside you but you don't really know it.

'Now that your tummy is full, Rahh, I think we should rest a little. It is a lovely morning and we should not rush.'

Rahh made sounds of contented agreement and twitched his whiskers again, pushing his nose further into the grass, as if to say – I have settled for the day.

16

All Waters Must Flow

After a period of contented rest, Golden Rabbit thought the time had come to speak again.

'Now then Rahh,' she said gently, so as not to shock the little bunny from his drifting thoughts on this summer's day. 'What was I asking you before we went chasing the truth about the roaring lion? Can you recall?'

'Oh Golden Rabbit, that seems such a long time ago now. I think I have been in a dream beneath the Great Light in the blue and now I need to wake up. Erm, I think you were asking me about the green grass,' said Rahh. 'Yes, you asked me was the grass different today?'

'Yes, that's right; and is it, Rahh?'

'I don't think so,' replied Rahh, thinking that there was a tricky comment coming any minute now to prove him wrong again.

There was silence for a short while, and Rahh wondered whether he should lie on his back like Golden Rabbit, looking into the blue. Then she spoke.

'All beings are funny creatures. They are blind for the most part, yet their eyes can see... but the truth can be tricky to see sometimes. The truth shimmers between worlds and you have to learn how to catch it as it flies past you. The world is full of illusion and delusion, and truth can only be seen by those who truly want to find it. You must seek it with all of your heart.'

'For most animals, especially the two-leggeds and the ones who think they are very clever, the truth watches them walk past it time and time again. It watches with every Great Light that rises into the blue in the morning and each moon that sails like a ship of gentle promises across the dark heaven when the Great Light sleeps,' said Golden Rabbit.

'You eat grass every day, Rahh, and mostly it seems the same to you – is that right?' she questioned.

'Yes,' said Rahh. 'It is more or less the same. The shades are a little lighter or darker and its sweetness changes with the seasons, but more or less, it is the same.'

Golden Rabbit rolled over onto her belly and looked into Rahh's eyes so deeply that he felt it inside him.

'Rahhhhhh,' she said, sounding like the lion roaring in his dream, both powerful and gentle at the same time. The sound penetrated him to the core, waking him from feeling comfortable and cosy with his full belly.

'I will show you the truth of what you have been eating for your breakfast all of your life. I will show you the truth, which most eyes do not see. I will show you the love that you eat with your breakfast grass every single day.'

'The *love* that I eat?' questioned Rahh.

'Oh yes,' replied Golden Rabbit. 'It is the gift from your Mother, but you can only see it when your Father shines his light upon it for you.'

Rahh was feeling very awake all of a sudden. Golden Rabbit could sense his questions coming and so she stayed silent.

'Golden Rabbit?' said Rahh, with a question in his voice. She continued to stay silent.

'Golden Rabbit, this morning seems to be very burdensome. It was like I entered a different world. There is too much to learn in this new world, and I am just a rabbit.'

'Yes, Rahh, that is what you said to me earlier this morning, but life is short and you have much to see. Time is so short, so very short for all rabbits and all other beings too. If only they could see how truly short it is, then they would not waste a

[67]

moment – but they do. In fact, a great many of them waste whole lives going nowhere: but you, Rahh, are different. You are special. You came here to learn.'

Rahh listened carefully to Golden Rabbit's wise words, then he felt that he must ask his burning questions.

'We entered the Field of Wonders and you spoke about my mother and father and I was supposed to eat a Light breakfast and now you tell me I have eaten love for breakfast instead. I didn't see any lights in the Field of Wonders. Did I not eat a Light breakfast then? Did the light not come and did the love come instead?'

Golden Rabbit reached out her front paw and placed it on Rahh's in a loving way. He remembered the first time she had done this: it was when he was missing his brothers and sisters and the touch of her paw melted his pain away. It was the same again in this moment. He was not worried, confused or lonely anymore, but he did feel full up with so many new ideas that he was having trouble trying to understand.

'Light and love are the same thing, Rahh,' explained Golden Rabbit. 'Animals just use different names to mean the same thing, and yes, I know that can be confusing.'

'Mother and Father are the Earth and the blue above our heads. Well, beyond the blue really, the whole Heavens, and the Field of Wonders is what you can make of your life when you learn to see truth. You walk upon your Mother, and your Father offers to guide your steps with his Heavenly light. If you can feel the pulse of their hearts within you, then you will be guided along your path, Rahh.'

'When you entered this field, it was just like an ordinary field of grass to you, but now you know that you walk upon your Mother and your Father looks down upon you with his grace. He is full of care for you. You are loved into life by them both. Your life is the blessing that comes from Mother and Father working together to create you. Their light beats like the thumping feet of rabbits, in your chest. That is the sign of your life within you,' said Golden Rabbit.

'You think you ate grass for breakfast, but really you ate light and love. I will show you.'

'Let us move to a place where we have not trodden the grass.'

The rabbits hopped to a fresh part of the field and then Golden Rabbit stood with her back to the Great Light in the blue, so that it shone over her shoulder, falling upon the grass in front of her.

She said, 'Rahh, most rabbits and other beings cannot see beyond their whiskers, but right there in front of you are the richest, brightest jewels you will ever see. They are yours for the taking. Mother and Father offer them to you every day, but hardly anyone sees this wealth and even fewer give thanks for it.'

Rahh looked carefully, but all he could see was grass. Golden Rabbit knew that he couldn't see it yet because he was not looking in the right way.

Golden Rabbit spoke again. 'Stop looking, and see instead.'

'How do you do that, Golden Rabbit?' said Rahh. 'How can you stop looking and see at the same time?'

'Let your eyes go misty Rahh and then look with the beating heart in your centre. Look carefully at the grass, Rahh, and then tell me what lies upon it.'

Rahh looked carefully and the only thing he could see was that the grass was still a little wet with the morning dew.

Rahh said, 'The only thing I can see is that the grass has some morning wetness on it from the cold dark time.'

'Yes,' said Golden Rabbit. 'Now stand with your back to the Great Light in the blue, so that it shines over your shoulder and falls upon the morning dew. Now look very carefully into a single drop of water and tell me what you see.'

Rahh concentrated and looked deeply into an arching blade of grass, weighed down with the dewy moisture. He focused his eyes on a single drop of dew. His attention was drawn to the warmth of the Great Light in the blue behind him, and just at that moment, the light hit his eye. It was the brightest green light he had ever seen.

He blinked hard and jumped backwards. 'By my longest whiskers!' he said, with both shock and excitement in his voice. 'Golden Rabbit, I saw it. I saw it! Just for a second, even less than a second, it was a jewel so bright and it touched me inside; the brightest green light I have ever, ever seen! I felt it touch me! I felt it deep inside me,' said Rahh in excited disbelief.

Golden Rabbit smiled at him. She didn't say a word. This was his moment to savour. This was the first time he had seen the gift of life, given by Mother and illuminated by Father. This was the pinpoint of Light and Love in the water of life.

Rahh suddenly found that he could not speak. Something was happening inside him. He became dizzy, but also felt that he was expanding; growing in some way. He felt pressure building up in his body, like he was going to burst.

Golden Rabbit remained silent. She rolled over onto her back and looked up into the blue, resting herself.

Rahh was trying to speak and it seemed like a whole day had passed before he could get a word out.

He began to slowly tremble and then shake, and eventually, words came out of him.

'G-o-l-d-e-n R-a-b-b-i-t?' he croaked, as he trembled.

'Yes Rahh,' she replied.

'I saw it Golden Rabbit. I…I…I saw the Light.'

Rahh couldn't hold the pressure in his body any longer. Suddenly, without warning he burst into tears. He lowered his chin to the ground between his paws, completely exhausted. Tears flooded from his little eyes, running down his fur onto his paws. He sobbed and sobbed so deeply with no idea why. He had just seen the most amazing and beautiful emerald light and now he couldn't speak for the pain inside his body.

Golden Rabbit rolled over and reached out, placing her paw on Rahh's.

'Let the water flow from your eyes, Rahh. All waters must flow.'

Rahh sobbed deeply for quite some time before he could speak again, and even then it was so hard to even find a single word.

'I don't know why I am crying,' he said. 'I don't understand it, Golden Rabbit. What happened to me? I saw this most beautiful jewel in the grass and something happened inside me.'

'Yes,' said Golden Rabbit. 'Now you must listen to your own words carefully, because that is where you will find the truth.'

'Most beings don't even hear their own words, they are just sounds that spill from their flapping mouths, but your mouth is full of truth right at this moment and so you must listen carefully to your own words and live by them. Do not live by the words of others, but live by your own words and the experiences of what you have seen.'

Golden Rabbit put her paw to Rahh's cheek and collected a single rabbit tear. She held it up beneath the Great Light in the blue and said to Rahh, 'This is your water of life Rahh. Look into this tear and tell me what you see.'

Rahh tried to focus his watery eyes as he twitched his nose and whiskers, then there it was again, the piercing light, but this time ruby red. It hit him deep inside and again the great pressure burst forth in a flood of tears with sobbing even deeper than before. He rolled onto his side in the warm grass, exhausted and his legs ran as if he was in a deep dream. Golden Rabbit lay close to comfort him with her warm body. There was a great pain inside him that he didn't understand.

Golden Rabbit hummed a tune softly and put a paw on Rahh's shoulder.

'Let it all go, Rahh. Let it all flow.'

'Like the waterfall of life tumbling over the cliff of destiny. Let it all go Rahh, let it all go.'

'All waters must flow Rahh, Let it all go.'

17

Seeing the Light

The rabbits lay in the grass as the Great Light in the blue passed the mid-point and began to fall towards the Mother, as it did at the end of each cycle. Rahh had slipped into a deep, healing sleep and Golden Rabbit remained next to him.

It was getting cooler and a chilly breeze woke Rahh as it ruffled his fur. He lay there stiller than still, not really knowing where he was for a moment.

He flicked his whiskers and thought to himself, 'I am confused, but that is ok because I'm just a rabbit. But something has changed inside me and I don't know what it is.'

He thought about Golden Rabbit's words: 'Listen to your own words. Listen to your own truth.' Then his little body jumped a little and he rolled onto his feet and turned his head to look at Golden Rabbit.

She was smiling at him. 'How do you feel, little bunny?' she asked.

'Yes, I'm fine,' said Rahh. 'I am a fine rabbit,' he said, with a smile on his face. 'But I think I am different. Something is different inside me.'

'Did you feel the pain, Rahh?' asked Golden Rabbit.

'Yes, there was so much pain inside me, but now it is gone and I am lighter,' he replied.

'When the water flows from your eyes it washes the pain away. Your pain leaves your broken body,' Golden Rabbit explained.

'But my body is only young, Golden Rabbit; it is not broken,' Rahh puzzled.

'All beings are broken inside, until the inside changes,' said

Golden Rabbit. 'They carry the pain of life whilst looking for life. When they see the light for the first time, the pain begins to come and is released through the tears. The tears are born through the pressure when something changes inside you. Then the waters of life flow.'

'Birth is always painful, Rahh. It is the transition from one place to another. Birth is when you arrive in a new place. Death is the leaving of one place and the arrival in the next. Sometimes that place is here with the rabbits, born into the burrow of the mother; and sometimes it may be with the winged ones who surge into the blue without a care in the world. We come and we go, and each time we return it is to learn how to change and grow into the next expression of our perfect, special selves.'

'This morning, your next birth began when you saw something that you never saw before, yet you ate it every morning. You saw the light of the father reflected in the jewels of the mother, who lays them out every morning for your breakfast. This birth is like changing your winter fur for your summer fur, Rahh – but the change is inside you and it is permanent. You cannot go back to that other life once you have seen the light. You are now a changed rabbit,' said Golden Rabbit.

Rahh said, 'I can't explain it, but I felt the change.'

'Yes,' said Golden Rabbit. 'You have "the knowing" that something has changed. It is a wonderful experience that nobody can ever take away from you. You must treasure the memory and the feelings of this morning, for this is the first time that you saw the light.'

'Thank you, Golden Rabbit,' said the little bunny.

'What are you thanking me for, Rahh?'

'I don't know, but I just need to say thank you. Something inside me needs to say thank you,' he replied.

'You are welcome Rahh. It is my great pleasure to serve you.'

Then she continued, 'Now, Rahh, it is getting cool and late. It is time for us to leave the Field of Wonders and go to the burrow.

[73]

Tonight you will sleep in my burrow so that you will not feel lonely. Is your body ready to move?'

'Yes, Golden Rabbit, I am ready. Thank you.'

The rabbits stretched their bodies and legs and pointed their whiskers to the blue, then slowly hopped from the Field of Wonders towards the dark, safe wood where their burrows lay.

18

Time to Rest

The rabbits made their way to the safety of the woodland and Golden Rabbit took Rahh to her burrow, which was beneath the roots of a great oak tree.

'Why do we not share a burrow, Golden Rabbit?' asked Rahh.

'There are times when I need to be alone, Rahh. There are many things a Golden Rabbit must do at different times to help Mother and Father. Occasionally, I can spend some time with another rabbit, but mostly I must be in my own space, on my own.'

'Do you not get lonely?'

'No, not at all,' Golden Rabbit reassured him. 'I am fulfilled deeply within. I am not alone inside, I am full of the light of love, and love is my constant companion. It is with me all of the time. Now, follow me down the burrow and we'll make ourselves comfortable for the night.'

As the rabbits went down the burrow, Rahh was surprised to see that it was lit as brightly as the daytime outside – not like his old burrow, which was dark. Golden Rabbit offered him a very comfortable place to lie down with soft, dry grass and some fresh green leaves in case he should be hungry or thirsty during the dark time.

As they settled in, Rahh felt a question coming that he had to ask before going to sleep.

Of course, Golden Rabbit was expecting it.

'Golden Rabbit,' said Rahh. 'What happened to me this morning when I saw the light? Why did the tears flow from my eyes?'

'This morning, I was your Guide,' replied Golden Rabbit. 'A

Guide is one who knows the way. A Guide is a bringer of light to others. So, this morning I guided you to see what you could not see or experience for yourself. I guided you to the place where the light could touch you. Then you experienced it for yourself. It is hidden in plain sight of all beings that walk this earth, but not many see it.'

'Sometimes a Guide must explain things to you in many ways until you can see the truth for yourself. If I just told you that each morning when you eat breakfast you eat light, love and emerald green jewels, then you would think I was a crazy rabbit. But when you can see and feel the truth of it for yourself, then your life changes and you have the knowing. Once you know something at such a deep level you know the truth.'

'All beings find their way to the light eventually and when it touches them their life begins to change. Their friends who haven't yet seen the light think they have become crazy,' chuckled Golden Rabbit. 'But there is no choice, Rahh. The light changes you. It awakens you to the truth of many things that others do not see but also, it can be a lonely path initially. You are often on your own, until there is enough light in you that you no longer need any other being in the world. Contentment comes with knowing that you are not alone; you are served every moment by mother and father, and the skill is to be in alignment with them, which of course means being out of alignment with some of the other creatures in this world.'

'Most beings are aware that there is a great spirit or a great light that works above us and alongside us, but if you say to them that you have actually seen it, then they think you are a mad rabbit!' Golden Rabbit laughed again.

'The world is a very funny place, Rahh. The more light you see, the funnier it becomes, because most of the beings are running around with their eyes totally closed even though they are actually open. They just can't see the truth through them until they have had an experience like you had this morning.'

[76]

'Let us rest for the night and tomorrow we will go to the Field of Wonders again, and I will explain to you exactly what happened to you. Now make yourself comfortable on this lovely soft grass that we are so lucky to have Rahh, and say a little prayer of thanks. Tonight you will rest deeply and you may dream of the most important of rabbit things, like being filled with joy in the early morning as the green, loving grass fills your belly and the Great Light in the blue warms your fur. Life is as simple and joyful as we make it for ourselves, Rahh.'

Golden Rabbit lay on her soft bed of dry grass not too far away from Rahh and the bright light in the burrow began to fade. Even before it had gone completely, Rahh's whiskers relaxed and he was already in a deep sleep.

Golden Rabbit looked at this brave little bunny with love in her eyes for the great journey ahead of him. She twitched her whiskers, which sent a blessing into his heart.

'Goodnight, sweet and gentle rabbit,' she whispered. 'Sleep in peace.'

19

The Zzard

Morning came soon enough. Rahh was awake early but he lay still on his bed of grass with his eyes closed, thinking to himself how lucky he was to have a friend like Golden Rabbit. She was so wise and full of teaching and all the lessons he learned were so fascinating. He thought again about his brothers and sisters living their lives, doing the same thing day after day and here he was with a great wise rabbit. He had no idea how that had happened or what it all meant, but he was very, very sure that he was in the right place. He could feel the truth of it.

Eventually he opened his eyes and saw that the burrow was quite dark. Although he had felt the presence of Golden Rabbit whilst he had been thinking, she was not actually there. He pricked up his ears, lifted himself onto his front legs and began to move to the entrance of the burrow. The pink light of the early morning was trickling towards him as he peeped his nose out into the cool air. He sniffed its fragrance and twitched his whiskers to see if it was safe to come out.

'Good morning, Rahh!' shrieked an unfamiliar voice. Rahh took a step back down the burrow and opened his eyes wide. Suddenly the air was filled with a whistling sound: '*Wheeees, wheeees, wheees!*'

'Good morning!' came the voice again. 'You may come out, it is safe.' Rahh pushed his whiskers towards the entrance and peered out but couldn't see anyone.

'Up here, Rahh,' the voice called.

Rahh looked up – and saw a great winged Zzard with a razor-sharp beak and talons like curved knives. He was instantly filled with terror at the sight and shot back down the burrow. He hid his head beneath the soft grass of his bed as his fur trembled with fear.

'What am I going to do?' he thought. 'I can't get out. And where is Golden Rabbit? Has she been killed and eaten by the Zzard? Oh my, oh no, what will I do?'

The Zzard was now on the ground and at the entrance to the burrow.

'Good morning, Rahh,' he called in his shrieking voice. '*Wheeees, wheeees, wheees.*'

Rahh knew that sound well. He had seen a great Zzard swoop from the blue one morning and carry off a small rabbit. All the other rabbits ran as fast as the rain to their burrows and didn't come out for three cycles of the Great Light. They all shook in terror at what they had seen.

Rahh felt the lion coming up from his belly. His whiskers began to tremble and before he knew it, his body jumped and he ran towards the entrance of the burrow as roaring words shot forth from his lips, shaking his whole body.

'Stand back from my house, you great beast, or I will bring the dragon fire from my belly and singe your fine feathers,' he roared.

Rahh was now trembling with the sound of his own voice as well as his fear.

From the entrance to the burrow a great laughing sound came tumbling down towards him.

'Hahaha, you dragon rabbit,' laughed the Zzard. 'My feathers are trembling with the fear of ten rabbits! Now come on out, Rahh. It is safe. I am here to watch over you whilst Golden Rabbit has gone to the Field of Wonders.'

'How do I know this is not a trick?' shouted Rahh.

'If I tell you a secret that only you know, then will you believe that it is safe?' asked the Zzard.

'Speak your words then, Zzard, and I will feel if you speak truthfully.'

'*Wheeees, wheeees, wheees,*' began the Zzard . . .

'Listen now
Rabbit low
Underground
Down below.
I will tell you, I will tell you
What you need to know.'

The Zzard spoke slowly. 'Today, little rabbit, you are not on my menu, because something special has happened to you. You have seen the green light and it touched the flower that beats like a drum inside your fur. All those who have seen the green light know each other by their sign.'

'What is that sign?' shouted Rahh, not knowing what it was himself.

'The sign is the way your love glows and flows into the world, Rahh,' answered the Zzard.

Rahh thought to himself, 'But I don't glow. I am just a rabbit, although I am a special rabbit and I am not quite the same rabbit that I was yesterday. I am different, and this morning I have felt the lion within me that was in my dream; and some kind of crazy words about dragon fire spoke through my whiskers. Mmmm. Perhaps all of this is a part of the sign? Perhaps the dragon fire glows?'

At that thought, he heard Golden Rabbit humming a morning tune full of green light. Rahh panicked and thought to himself that the great Zzard would eat her.

He called to the lion inside him, but it didn't seem to be there. He called to the dragon fire that would singe the feathers of the great Zzard, but that wasn't there either. Then he heard the call of the Zzard.

'*Wheeees, wheeees, wheees,*' it cried, and there came a thunderous noise of giant wings beating by the entrance to the burrow, as it rose towards the blue.

Rahh had visions of Golden Rabbit being lifted into the blue, clutched in the razor-like talons of the Zzard.

[80]

Suddenly his legs thrust him up the burrow and the roaring lion thundered through his whiskers once again.

'Look out Golden Rabbit, a Zzard is above you! Look out, run for the burrow. Quickly. Quickly!'

'Rahh,' came Golden Rabbit's soft voice. 'I hear you are awake.' The lion's roar rattled Rahh's whiskers again.

'Golden Rabbit, be careful – there is a great Zzard waiting to eat us. Quickly, run down the burrow.'

Rahh heard the Zzard's call again and the beating of the massive wings. But then he heard Golden Rabbit laugh.

'Rahh, it is fine. It's ok. The Zzard is here to watch over you. He is our friend and guardian. All is well, you may come out.'

Rahh, still trembling, didn't know what to think, but it was clear that Golden Rabbit had not been eaten or taken into the blue. He crept gingerly up the burrow until he could see Golden Rabbit speaking with the Zzard just outside. As Rahh approached, they both laughed and Golden Rabbit put out her paw to Rahh to show it was safe.

Already, Rahh was not yet out into the world this morning, and he was confused and terrified. How could rabbits have a Zzard as a friend? This was not what he understood to be safe. All rabbits know that Zzards eat rabbits for breakfast.

'At last, good morning Rahh,' said the Zzard, and Rahh hesitatingly returned the greeting.

'You are a brave and wise rabbit, Rahh,' said the Zzard, laughing heartily, 'and with a voice like thunder for such a small rabbit. My feathers fair trembled and shook me to my bones!'

'Let me tell you Golden Rabbit,' said the Zzard, 'Rahh roared at me like a lion and said that he would bring the dragon fire from his belly to singe my fine feathers. He is such a brave, brave soul. But how does he know about the dragon fire, Golden Rabbit?'

'I have not taught him about the dragon fire yet,' she answered; 'he must have learned of it through the petals of his opening heart flower, whilst in the warmth of the rabbit dream world. But we will find this out later. For now, we have breakfast to eat and work to do, the work that is not yet finished from yesterday. Will you fly the sacred patterns in the blue for us today, Zzard, so that we may spend time in the Field of Wonders without a care?'

'It will be my pleasure, Golden Rabbit. It is a fine day for flying the sacred circles of light, as the air is already warming from the Great Light in the blue. I shall stretch my feathers wide and perhaps see you later in the day.'

'Thank you Zzard,' said Golden Rabbit, and the great winged creature launched himself towards the blue, calling his strange cry as he went.

Rahh looked bewildered. He had never seen anything like a rabbit and a Zzard speaking with each other. Already he was exhausted from the rabbit fear, the roaring lion, the dragon fire and the confusion of a great winged terror-beast greeting the morning with gentle rabbits.

'Oh no,' he thought. 'If I am only just out of my bed and all this has happened, what will the rest of the day hold? I'm only a small rabbit, it is all too much.'

Golden Rabbit sensed Rahh's disturbance and couldn't help chuckling beneath her whiskers. Indeed, it must have been a terrible fright for Rahh but at least it woke him up, she thought.

'Well, young Rahh, are you ready for some breakfast?'

Rahh looked at Golden Rabbit and no words would come out of his mouth.

Golden Rabbit could see that he was beyond words at this moment.

'Follow me to the Field of Wonders and soon your belly will be full of light, love and sweet juicy grass and you will be restored to your fine and best self.'

Golden Rabbit smiled, turned and hopped towards the edge of the wood as Rahh followed silently behind her.

20

Flower of Life

Golden Rabbit led the way to the edge of the wood and peered through the fence waiting. Rahh stopped and looked into the field, and wondered what Golden Rabbit was waiting for.

He asked, 'What are we waiting for, Golden Rabbit?'

'I am waiting for permission to walk upon the sacred ground,' said Golden Rabbit.

'Is this the Field of Wonders that we were in yesterday?'

'Yes,' said Golden Rabbit, waiting for Rahh's next question.

'Do you have to ask permission to enter the field today then, Golden Rabbit?'

'Every day I ask permission, Rahh, and at the end of each day I give thanks and I'm full of gratitude for each step that I was allowed to take on this sacred and holy ground. Now, let us pass beneath the fence and find a nice place to eat breakfast.'

Golden Rabbit could feel Rahh's many questions rising up into his whiskers, desperate to burst out into the world and she chuckled to herself. 'What a wonderful little rabbit, wanting to know so much, seeking the answers to everything beneath the Great Light in the blue.'

Golden Rabbit led Rahh to a lovely place where the Great Light in the blue tumbled upon the fresh green grass. All around there was a wall of tall grass so that they could not be seen. It was like they were in a kind of open-air burrow, safe and secure from the world outside. There was also a small bush to provide shade if the Great Light in the blue began to burn very bright and hot.

'Now then, Rahh, I know you have many questions this morning, especially about the Zzard but I must speak to you about yesterday and what happened to you when you looked into the water of life and saw the jewels of Mother and Father. Eat some of the beautiful green grass now, Rahh but ask permission first and give thanks afterwards. I will rest for a while on my back, gazing into the blue and from time to time I will help you to see the truth.'

'Thank you Golden Rabbit,' said Rahh, and he began to eat.

Golden Rabbit hummed one of her little tunes to help Rahh feel relaxed and let him know that he could eat his fill in peace. As Rahh tasted mouthful after mouthful of rabbit breakfast Golden Rabbit felt him becoming very satisfied with the feelings of his full tummy. Presently Rahh was ready to listen and to hear.

'How do you feel, Rahh?' asked Golden Rabbit.

'Mmm, I feel very rabbity. My fur is glowing and my whiskers are strong,' he replied. He stretched his front legs out before him and put his nose down between his paws. 'I am very *furry*, Golden Rabbit,' he said.

Golden Rabbit rolled over on to her belly and looked deeply into Rahh's eyes.

'Do you know the thumping inside your fur, Rahh?'

'Yes, I feel it strongly when I run in fear,' said Rahh.

'The thumping is your heart at the centre of your being. It is like a flower of a thousand petals; our work is to open the petals one at a time to reveal the truth of who you are at the centre,' said Golden Rabbit.

'You are my student, and I will teach you about your heart, Rahh.'

'Your heart is like a rosebud in a spring garden, the petals all tightly bound in a ball, hiding the beauty that will eventually emerge. A little at a time the water of life falls around the feet of the rose bush and the Great Light in the blue touches the bud. With these gifts of water and light from Mother and Father, a petal begins to unfurl.'

'One by one the petals open until finally the great mother speaks through the rose.'

[84]

Rahh's eyes lit up with a question and Golden Rabbit lifted her paw to signal to him to wait. Then she continued.

'The Mother Earth sends up to the rose her love, which is the water of life, but it is a sweet and sticky water called nectar. When the nectar arrives beneath the Great Light in the blue, the Mother sends forth beautiful music, like a fanfare to announce the arrival of the sweet water of life. But this is not music that you hear with your ears, Rahh, it is music that you smell with your nose. It is the most beautiful scent that plays its tune to the air that we breathe. Then the greatest, wisest creatures come to listen and the beauty of the musical notes touches their hearts. The music tells the wise creatures that the water of life from the Mother is ready for them. They fly on wings of gossamer gold and alight within the heart of the rose to feed.'

'What are these wise creatures Golden Rabbit?'

'They are the golden bees, that sing when they fly,' she said.

'When the water of life and the music burst into the world, the Mother offers a golden yellow powder of love, which in turn, will create more flowers. The powder is bright like the Great Light in the blue and it shines forth from the heart of the rose. The wise creatures make a wonderful music of their own when they approach the flower – a humming sound that fills the summer air. Then they land upon the rose and bathe in the scent of beautiful music whilst they feed. Their hearts open and are filled with joy from these gifts of the Mother. The wise creatures become full of light and work hard at being creators of light, playing in this great game of love.'

'The nectar and music show the wise creatures how to share the golden yellow love-powder in the world. Their hearts overflow with love and joy and they join in this divine game by taking the golden yellow love-powder to other flowers whilst singing their beautiful song with their wings.'

Rahh's eyes were wide with astonishment and his mouth was open as he listened to every word that Golden Rabbit spoke.

She continued.

'As the Great Light in the blue shines down on their beautiful wings, they are reminded to take some of this love home with them, which they turn into a thick, sticky liquid that is called honey. The two-leggeds also call the ones they love by that same name – honey – for when any two creatures come together in the great light of love it is a very sweet engagement of Flowers of Life.'

'So, Rahh, the Mother sends forth the water of life; and the Father who commands the Great Light in the blue shines that light upon her waters and so water and light then create all things that bring love into the world.'

'The rose is like your heart, Rahh. It is the Flower of Life at your centre. It shows you its petals and how they open. It shows you the beautiful music of love and the sweetness of the nectar of love. All love makes hearts open and then open hearts can bring more love into the world, just as the open rose brings more love into the world.'

'All creatures that can fly or walk or swim or crawl or move in any kind of way can bring love into the world if they have an open heart.'

'Do you understand, Rahh?'

'Yes, I think so,' said Rahh.

'Love is at the centre of everything,' said Golden Rabbit. 'Love is the light that brings forth itself into the world. Love brings light and light brings love and they are both the same at the same time. So, when you see the rose you know that it is like your heart and that there is love and light at the centre and that love and light are always trying to burst into the world. As each petal opens, the love and the light push harder to be seen.'

Golden Rabbit bent her head and took a blade of grass into her mouth and chewed for a moment or two before continuing.

'Yesterday, Rahh, I brought you into this Field of Wonders and

[86]

showed you the grass in a way that you had never seen it before. I showed you the water of life and you saw the treasure inside the water that Mother and Father had brought for you.'

'When you saw the light in the water of life for the first time, it touched your heart and the power of it was so intense that it burst open your heart at a deep level.'

'Some petals then opened and the waters of life flowed from your eyes, carrying forth the pain that was hidden within you. That is why a teacher is sent to you when you are ready, Rahh or sometimes you are sent to the teacher. The teacher knows how to touch your heart with light and in that process your heart opens like the rose full of beautiful music, nectar and love. Once a petal opens, Rahh, it can never close again. It is a process that we call 'emerging into light', but really it is your own light emerging into you. It is a process of constant opening until all the petals are fully open and all your light that is hidden behind the petals comes forth and shines into the world. You become the light that is within you and the light becomes you. Just like the light is love and the love is light. You become everything and everything becomes you and you shine brighter than the Great Light in the blue, and with each opening petal comes more wisdom.

'When you begin to seek the light then it will respond and show itself to you; but if you do not seek it, it may remain hidden forever. The light only comes forth and touches those who truly seek it with all of the light in their heart. It only comes forth to those who have great desire to experience the love of Mother and Father. It only comes forth for those who desire to understand the light that is beyond all light. When the light in the drop of water touches you deeply in the heart then a petal opens. As light emerges from behind each petal it lights our path and our way and that is how we make the journey of life through this world, Rahh.'

'When the waters of life flow from our eyes, then the pain

leaves our broken bodies and we become more whole, even though it seems like we are whole anyway. The pain is caused as the light opens the petals.'

Golden Rabbit finished speaking and Rahh knew that the teaching was finished, or at least the words were finished.

Golden Rabbit continued to look into Rahh's eyes and he felt the light from her touching his heart. He sat, bathed in her music of love as the Great Light in the blue bowed its head towards them, warming their bodies with the rays of love.

The rabbits remained like this for some time, as if in a kind of waking sleep, gazing into each other's eyes without moving. Time passed and the Great Light in the blue began to fall towards the Mother and the day began to cool.

In the stillness of love, a sound pierced the air. '*Wheeees, wheeees, wheeees,*' and the shadow of a great dragon passed over them. Rahh looked up to see the Zzard wheeling through the blue. Golden Rabbit said, 'Our day is now complete.'

21

Bran

That night Rahh went to his own burrow. It was time for Golden
Rabbit to be alone in her world. The burrow was lovely as usual,
and filled with light. Tomorrow would be a new day but for now
Rahh was very satisfied. He was comfortable. He felt loved and
full of love, which also meant that he was full of light.

He settled on the soft, dry grass and put his nose between his
paws. Immediately, his mind began to let go as sleepiness washed
through him.

There was a warmth in the burrow that took him far, far away.
A memory of long ago flashed through his thoughts. A field that
he used to know with rabbits and a life that he used to know, but
now everything was different. He felt the rose growing inside his
fur, beating with the light that Golden Rabbit had poured into
him through her eyes. Tomorrow was such a long way away but
yesterday was even further. The past was the past and none of it
mattered any longer. As it began to drift from his memory a dark
image started to appear in front of him.

Two yellow eyes shone out of the darkness and a dark shape
with the armour of a soldier entered the burrow. Rahh was suddenly awake again and kept perfectly still, trying not to be seen
but yet he wasn't frightened. The yellow eyes continued to stare
at him as he lay low and looked back at them.

'Hello Rahh,' said a deep voice in an accent from long ago.
Rahh said nothing and kept still. The eyes began to move to the
side of him so that he had to turn his head to follow them. They
stopped and the voice spoke again.

'Did you feel the pain yesterday, Rahh? Did you feel the pain as you lay in the grass and the waters of life flowed from your eyes?'

Rahh kept silent as he did not know what to make of those yellow eyes.

'I am Bran, a great warrior from the past. I am here to thank you, Rahh. Yesterday you set me free when the pain left your body. I was trapped inside you from a long, long time ago. From many, many lives ago.'

'As a great warrior I fought in battles and sometimes I hurt innocent creatures because of the darkness and anger within me. We all have the darkness and it is our work to let it out so that it does not harm others. Sometimes we cause pain with our careless thoughts and actions. Yes, a single thought can hurt another, even if it is not spoken. When we hurt others we gather pain inside ourselves, and that pain remains within us lifetime after lifetime, after lifetime, until we find the light that will let the pain out as the waters of life flow.'

'I am Bran, the shadow of all the things you have done in the past, Rahh; all the things that were not full of love and wholesome in your desires.'

Rahh listened to every word as the yellow eyes continued to gaze at him.

'Tonight is the darkest night of the cycle, Rahh – before the silver moon is newly born in the heavens once more. This is a great time to shed the darkness of your shadow, before the light of the new moon comes to show you a new journey of life. A rebirth! So I come to you in darkness with only the light in my eyes for you to see. The rest of me must remain in shadow as my darkness dissolves back into earth as Mother helps to cleanse me.'

'I come this night in shadow to give thanks, Rahh. You have my deepest thanks for having the great courage of the warrior rabbit.'

At this, Rahh finally spoke. 'But I am not a warrior rabbit, I am just a rabbit.'

'You are not what you think you are, Rahh,' replied Bran. 'You are what is inside you. You have the courage of the lion in your heart. The greatest warriors are those who fight the battle to open their hearts, not those who hurt others. We have been in those other battles together, in the past, Rahh, where our thoughts have hurt others. The past is over now, it is finished. Now we are moving into light from the shadows of our older lives. We have been given another chance on this Earth to find a new way and to walk in the way of light with Mother and Father to help us.'

'Yesterday, as the pain left your body you set me free; and today, as I walk free from the dark things we did in older times, you will become lighter and freer too. More pain will leave you and you will learn to fly in the heart. Your heart will become full of joy, full of light and full of the gift of being able to see more than those who are still trapped inside themselves.'

'As the morning comes, your life will be full of light. Then you will need your courage to see how to carry it into the world.'

'Now, Rahh, my wings are growing to allow me to leave this Earth and go back to the Father, where he will prepare me for my next journey as a glorious creature on this fine Earth. We will meet again as greater beings than before. We will carry the banner of light before our open hearts and we will soothe the pain of those who seek our help. Sleep well and give thanks for all that you experience, for each breath will bring a new world into you, if you allow it.'

'Farewell, Rahh. I bless you with my growing golden wings. You are now free of the dark shadow that you carried in your heart.'

The yellow eyes slipped back into the darkness and disappeared. Rahh remained on his bed wondering what part of himself was this older, darker self – the warrior who had just left?

The burrow still felt warm and comfortable and as Rahh considered all that Bran had spoken of he slipped into a restful sleep.

22

The Silent Dawn

As Rahh awoke, the burrow was cool – chilly even – and the light seemed low. He stretched his legs and pointed his whiskers into the air as he thought about Bran, the shadow who had visited in the night: was he the reason for the lack of light this morning?

Suddenly, a piercing cry split the air. '*Wheeees, wheeees, wheeees*! Rahh, come quickly!' shouted Zzard.

Rahh ran up the burrow to see Zzard perched on a high branch of the old oak tree just outside the burrow.

'What is it, Zzard?' he shouted, his whiskers pointing to the sky.

'The wood is changed,' Zzard replied. 'There is no light. Golden Rabbit cannot be found anywhere.'

Rahh thought to himself, 'So, is this what the darkness is, and the chilly burrow? Is it because Golden Rabbit is not here?' 'What do you mean,' he shouted back. 'How is the wood changed and where is Golden Rabbit?'

'This morning there was silence in the wood. I flew up to see what was happening. Nothing under the Great Light in the blue was glowing. There is a sadness in the earth, and the trees hang their leaves in pain,' said Zzard. 'I have spoken with other creatures and we think that Golden Rabbit has been taken from us. There is no golden light in the wood!'

'Have you looked for her?' asked Rahh.

'Yes, I have flown the highest circles and called upon all the feathered ones to fly everywhere in the wood; none can find a trace of Golden Rabbit. She has gone!'

Rahh felt a sudden pain in his heart. A great pain of loss. The world had gone dark and even the Great Light in the blue was hidden.

'What can we do, Zzard?' he cried. 'She can't be gone. What has happened to her? Come down from the tree. We must make a plan.'

Zzard flew down from his high branch and stood like a massive dragon in front of Rahh. Rahh felt no fear of this great winged creature as its breath ruffled his fur: he needed its help.

'She can't be far away. She must be underground or has taken a journey somewhere. She would not just leave without saying anything to us.'

Zzard replied, 'I have checked her burrow. Usually I can see her golden glow even when she is underground and there is no glow anywhere.'

'Can you take me into the blue in your great talons, Zzard, without hurting me?' asked Rahh.

'It might be possible,' said Zzard. 'If you have not had breakfast yet you will be light from sleep. I will try. Stand in front of me and put your ears under my beak and I will hold you beneath your belly.'

Rahh positioned himself beneath Zzard. There was a massive noise in his ears as Zzard beat his wings furiously. At first Rahh thought it wasn't going to work but then suddenly he was off the ground and moving at a great speed between the branches of the trees. The wind in his ears was like a great gale in the dark months and all his senses were dizzy as he moved in a way he had never moved before.

As they rose above the trees Rahh could see all the woodland below him, the ponds and the beautiful green Field of Wonders, the tall trees and the hedges under which they lay in the warm weather. He could see his whole world in a single view. It was truly wonderful and a vision of beauty.

'This is how we feathered ones fly each morning,' said Zzard.

'As soon as we are above the trees and high into the blue we can see the glow from Golden Rabbit. Even if she is in a burrow, the glow comes through the earth and she lights the whole world of our woodland heaven. This morning, we have been looking for her for hours, as you slept, but there is no sign of her.'

Zzard flew over the whole woodland with Rahh held carefully in his talons. It was a great experience for Rahh to fly above the trees like a winged creature but his excitement was tinged with worry and pain. Where was Golden Rabbit?

After flying above the wood in many circles and from a great height from which you could see everything, they returned to the glade where Rahh's burrow lay.

'I will look in Golden Rabbit's burrow,' said Rahh, and hopped a short distance and then down the burrow. Nothing. Not a sign of Golden Rabbit. The burrow was cold and damp. He came up to the surface again where Zzard was waiting for news.

'Nothing,' said Rahh. 'Not a sign of her. What shall we do?'

'This is terrible,' answered Zzard. 'I can hardly lift my wings. There is a great sadness throughout the wood. What shall we do?'

'Perhaps she had to go on a journey, suddenly,' said Rahh, hopefully.

They looked at each other and nodded in agreement. 'We should not worry too much,' said Rahh. 'All will be well, I am sure.'

'Yes, perhaps you are right, Rahh,' said Zzard. 'Let us not worry. Worry will get us nowhere. I will rest for a while and then fly the sacred circles again through the blue and see if can see the glow from Golden Rabbit.'

'Thank you, that is a wonderful thing to do,' said Rahh. 'In the meantime I will go to the Field of Wonders where she will know where to find me.'

Rahh hopped to the edge of the wood and looked through the fence into the Field of Wonders. He could not see any sign of Golden Rabbit. He asked permission of Mother to tread on her sacred earth and then gave thanks. Then he stepped into the field and went to the small bush where Golden Rabbit spent the days teaching him.

Rahh did all the things that they usually did together. He ate a Light breakfast and looked into the jewels hidden in the waters of life. He lay on his back looking into the blue. Occasionally, he would see Zzard flying his sacred circles. And as the Great Light in the blue began to fall towards Mother, he prepared to go back to the burrow for the night.

He tried not to worry but he also felt the loneliness and the emptiness of a world without Golden Rabbit's light.

Rahh went to the burrow and looked up into the darkening blue. He shouted good night to Zzard even though he could not see him: now Rahh knew that Zzard was indeed a good friend whom he could rely on. A *wheeees, wheeees* came back upon the breeze and then Rahh entered his burrow. His tummy was full. He was not hungry or thirsty and the grass was still soft even though there was a warmth missing from the burrow.

'I will try not to worry,' thought Rahh; and then he thought that the day had been very long, when normally it went very quickly. Even though he tried not to worry, the pain in his tummy was definitely a worrisome pain.

The following morning he was woken by Zzard calling again. Rahh ran up the burrow hoping for good news but Zzard looked at Rahh and shook his head in a sad way.

'There is no sign of her,' he said.

Rahh could see that Zzard's feathers looked a little dull.

'Are your feathers alright?' he asked.

'They are a little heavy,' Zzard replied. 'They feel heavy to lift. It seems that they are lacking a little energy.'

'My fur also feels a bit rough and also lacking something,' mused the bunny. Come with me to the Field of Wonders this morning, Zzard, and I will teach you how to drink the water of life from the green blades. Perhaps this will help your feathers.'

[95]

Thank you,' said Zzard. 'I will do that. I feel so heavy this morning and there is something strange inside me. It is an emptiness. When I fly into the blue I am normally full of joy but this morning there is a space where the joy should be.'

'Let me see can I help you,' said Rahh. 'Fly to the Field of Wonders where Golden Rabbit teaches me and we will eat together.'

Rahh bent his head to the earth as the great Zzard beat his wings to lift himself into the air then he ran towards the Field of Wonders.

23

Breakfast with Zzard

The Zzard was waiting for Rahh when he arrived after running across the field. Rahh sat down in front of him. He thought to himself that this was a strange scene: the Zzard was six times his size and towered above him like a great flying dragon. But yet he sat patiently waiting for Rahh to speak.

Rahh told the Zzard about the jewels of light in the water of life that lay upon the grass in the mornings. He tried to show him but the Zzard could not see the light. Rahh, however, could see it clearly and each time he saw a jewel it made his heart jump a little. Still, as much as he tried to show the Zzard, the great creature could not see it.

'Well, Zzard,' said Rahh. 'You have the most amazing eye-sight. You can see the tiniest thing from the highest point in the blue, but you cannot see the jewels of light in the water of life. I am confused and amazed. However, let us dine together. You may drink the water of life and I will eat the grass as usual and let us see if that helps your feathers.'

And so the pair breakfasted together until they were full.

Rahh said, 'This is when I have a lie down and rest. Usually you are flying the sacred circles to watch over me but today you are here in the Field of Wonders ... so, what shall we do?'

'I am ready to fly into the blue,' said the Zzard. 'I've spent a long time on the ground and now that I'm full of the waters of life that you showed to me, I must say that I feel better than I did this morning. Something is lifting and I would like to try out my feathers once more.'

The Zzard stretched out his great wings: they cast a shadow

over Rahh and he felt very small in front of this huge flying beast.

'Very well,' said the little bunny. 'Rise into the blue, Zzard, and fly your circles. Perhaps we will meet later in the day or next time the Great Light rises. If there is any news of Golden Rabbit I will call to you.'

'So be it,' replied the Zzard. 'Thank you for this great breakfast. I can indeed feel more strength in my wings, so whatever you showed me has worked even if I could not see it with my own eyes. I will see you later, Rahh. Rest and be happy. I will watch over you from above.'

The Zzard beat his wings against the air and launched himself towards the blue. Rahh rolled over and lay on his back watching the great dragon creature rise on the air until he was only a dot in the blue. He wondered why the Zzard could not see the jewels, even though he had the most amazing vision. Then he remembered something that Golden Rabbit had taught him.

As he lay quietly, he heard Golden Rabbit's voice on the wind. 'Only those who can see with their heart can see the jewels, Rahh. Only those whose time has come can see the light in the water of life. It is when you are ready for the becoming that your heart seeks the light. Only then can you see the love that Mother lays out for you each morning.'

Rahh's whiskers twitched. 'Yes, of course,' he thought. 'That is why the Zzard cannot see the jewels of light. Although he is a great and magnificent creature with incredible vision in his eyes, he is not yet ready to see with his heart.'

Rahh felt much better now that he had found the answer to the question that was puzzling him. Now, he felt like he could drift off to sleep and rest a little. He gazed up into the blue and there, a tiny dot swooped at a great speed across the blue and back again. Zzard was taking care of him.

Rahh drifted into a hazy sleep and the warmth of the Great Light touched his fur but he was aware that it was not as bright as when Golden Rabbit was here.

Rahh slept and dreamed. Occasionally he would hear Golden Rabbit's voice and open his eyes in relief, only to see that he was still alone in the Field of Wonders. All day long he drifted in and out of sleep, feeling that he really needed a deep, long rest.

Eventually, the Great Light rolled towards Mother Earth and the air cooled. Suddenly a shiver ran through him and a shadow covered the Great Light in the blue. It was the Zzard returning. He landed in front of Rahh and folded his great wings.

'Change is coming, Rahh,' he said. 'There is a chill wind blowing from the north. It has a bitter edge to it. I could feel it in my feathers as the Great Light began to fall towards mother.'

'Yes, I felt it too, Zzard. It was a chill that cut me deeply inside as your shadow folded across me.'

'This means that I must leave, Rahh. I cannot stay when the north wind comes, as it is too cold for my blood,' said the Zzard with some trepidation.

Rahh was saddened to hear this news as the creature had become a treasured companion. He sat up tall and pointed his ears to the blue. His whiskers stood out sharply in the cooling air and something inside him said, 'Time to rest in a deep burrow, Rahh.'

'You are right Zzard. Change is coming. I feel it too. If you must travel, then so be it. But I must say something first.'

'I must say that I have felt your friendship strongly in my whiskers. You have watched over me for a long time, day after day, and I ask you to accept my grateful thanks for this journey we have made together,' said Rahh. 'Where will you go?'

His friend replied, 'I must go where my feathers will be warmed in the early mornings so that I can rise into the blue. So I will go in the opposite direction to the cold wind.'

'When will you leave?' asked Rahh.

'I must leave on the first breath of warmth in the next rising of the Great Light, for the change will come quickly now,' said Zzard.

'So soon!' exclaimed Rahh, with some pain in his voice.

'I am afraid so. If I cannot soar into the blue then I will die. I must follow the light that warms the air to lift me.'

'Yes, I can see that,' said Rahh.

'I will walk with you to the burrow before the dark time comes,' said Zzard.

'Thank you. Yes, let us walk together,' said Rahh and they began to move towards the woodland.

As they approached the burrow, Rahh felt sad to be losing his great new friend who had helped him so much in looking for Golden Rabbit. Now he would be on his own again. The dark time was already upon them as they arrived at the burrow; somehow it seemed to be coming very quickly since Golden Rabbit had gone.

'I must rise into the trees now, Rahh, and so I must bid you goodbye as I may already have left when you rise on the morrow,' said Zzard.

'Yes,' said Rahh. 'You must go where the warmth and light are. You must look after your great feathers for they carry your whole life into the blue where the world sees your magnificence.'

'Rahh, take care of yourself. Keep your burrow warm and eat well. Perhaps it will not be long before Golden Rabbit returns.'

'Zzard, you are full of love and care, but I think we both know that Golden Rabbit has been taken from us by the creatures with great teeth, even though we dared not speak of such a thing,' said Rahh.

'It is true that we dared not speak of it, yes perhaps the wandering pack animals have taken her for food. I fear we will never know for sure. Take care, small rabbit. When I fly the sacred circles I will think of you each Great Light that rises in the dawn and at the song of the silver moon as she sails across the darkness with her promises of light to come. Take care, Rahh.'

'Goodbye, Zzard. Fly with care and may your feathers shine with the joy of flight and lift you into the love in the blue.'

The creatures had no more words but looked at each other for a moment; then the Zzard stretched out his powerful wings and Rahh bent his head as they cracked the air in front of him. The wonderful dragon-like creature lifted from the earth with a great cry: '*Wheeees, wheeees, wheeees!*'

Rahh watched him rise into the gathering dark time. Again he felt a chill run through him. He glanced over his shoulder to check that no other creatures were there and then dived down into the safety of his burrow.

24

Golden Rabbit's Burrow

Rahh awoke in the night. He could hear the north wind blowing around the entrance to his burrow. He felt his bones were getting colder and pulled the dry grass around his body.

The wind sang a song he didn't know – a song of emptiness and sorrow; of life slipping away. He listened to it carefully to hear its truth as Golden Rabbit had taught him, before slipping back into sleep where he saw visions of dark days to come. Of cold and loneliness. He saw himself embarking on a journey through endless white lands of bitterness.

Morning came soon enough and Rahh stretched his legs and began to hop up to the world outside. The north wind still blew and he saw the branches around the glade where the burrow lay thrashing in the wind. The leaves were being torn from them and all was dark above.

Rahh looked up to the blue, which wasn't blue any longer. There were no singing sounds from the feathered creatures and no call from the Zzard.

'How quickly life can change,' thought Rahh. 'Only yesterday I was trying to teach Zzard how to eat a Light breakfast and now it seems like a new world is suddenly emerging. A cold and bitterly empty world.'

Rahh went to the Field of Wonders and asked permission to enter. The wind blew the grass until it was almost flat and Rahh ran across the open space aware that the Zzard was not flying above him watching out for his safety. He came to the small bush that he had sat beneath with Golden Rabbit when the Great Light in the blue was too hot at the midpoint of the day;

already the leaves were being taken from it, rolling wildly across the ground.

He began to eat some breakfast grass, but it was different: in just one night the taste had left it. He could feel the juice nourishing him but the grass was bitter. This morning he didn't even look for the jewels in the water of life. He was concentrating on keeping warm as the north wind blew right through his fur and chilled his bones.

This morning he felt the loneliness. He felt the pain in his heart of losing Golden Rabbit, and now he had lost his friend Zzard; but at least he knew the great creature was safe and they had had a chance to say goodbye. Now there was just himself and the cold north wind.

Rahh took shelter beneath the bush and watched his world being blown away in front of him. All that he knew was being torn from the earth and sent flying through the air. He drew in his legs and tightened his shoulders, then laid his ears across his back and put his nose between his paws to keep it warm. His whiskers were weak and drooped as the wind whistled through the branches above his head.

'How life can change at the turn of the wind,' he thought. 'Once I was a small rabbit in a family and then I was a student with a great teacher. Then I lost my great teacher and companion and a great dragon creature helped me for a short time – and now he is gone too.'

'Now the north wind blows and my whole life is empty. Such is the life of a foolish rabbit that leaves his family,' he reflected sadly. 'Perhaps I should have stayed in the green garden and not gone on this adventure?'

Rahh watched the grey sky flying over his head and it seemed to be getting darker. Breakfast did not warm his bones this morning and he thought that he would be warmer and safer in the burrow. He pulled his legs and shoulders up tight and decided to run towards the woodland. In a second he was bolting across the earth towards the fence. As he entered the woodland he suddenly thought, 'Perhaps I will go to Golden Rabbit's burrow today.'

He hopped into the glade, passed his own burrow, went round the back of the great oak tree and entered Golden Rabbit's burrow. For some reason he thought it might be warmer or lighter or even feel better than his own, but to his disappointment it felt cold, empty and abandoned.

He looked around and the lovely bed of grass was damp but the burrow was a little bigger than his and so he decided that he would tidy up, find some new grass and make his home here for a while.

As the days passed, Rahh made his new burrow comfortable against the gathering cold. He liked the extra space of the high roof, which allowed him to sit up without his ears brushing the soil above. That way he didn't have to clean them quite so much each morning when he stepped outside.

As the cold wind continued, Rahh didn't go to the Field of Wonders any longer but rather nibbled at the small clumps of grass around the burrow and in the woodland nearby. He felt his world getting smaller and each day that went by the pain in his heart was more intense as he missed his life with Golden Rabbit.

One particularly dark night he was suddenly woken by a great flash of light rushing down his burrow, followed almost immediately by a crashing sound that shook the earth. Rahh had no idea what it was, but he didn't like it. It was fierce and his bones were frightened. All night long the north wind howled, water poured from the sky and the light continued to flash and the ground shake from the great crashing noise.

At one moment, in a flash of light he saw a rabbit he did not know at the entrance to his burrow. At first he thought that this must be a stranger looking for shelter from the fearsome storm. He was just going to bid it welcome when he noticed that it had no fur. There were no eyes, ears or whiskers either. Like the rabbits who had gone to the long rabbit sleep, it was just bones.

As it filled the entrance to his burrow Rahh began to fear that he was trapped. He backed up against the wall of the burrow looking at this strange creature blocking his escape. It looked right into Rahh's eyes with its lifeless, empty skull and was terrifying in its appearance.

'Get back,' shouted Rahh. 'Who are you? What do you want?'

As the rabbit began to speak its teeth rattled in its bony jaws.

'Rahh, I know who you are,' spoke the bones. 'Your winter is coming quickly and you may not see another Great Light for a long time. You may not ever see the Great Light in the blue again. You must take care of yourself, for there is no other rabbit on this earth can help you now, Rahh.'

'The white lands of bitterness are at your door and your heart will freeze with the pain of death. Nay, you may even call upon death to take you, and I will be waiting at the door.'

'Ask your Mother and Father to help you each day and keep yourself warm. You are alone in this place: no others can walk with you where you enter now.'

Another great flash of light shot down the burrow as the earth shook and rumbled, and the rabbit of bones was gone.

Rahh shook his head as these new fears flooded through him, and tears burst from his eyes as he put his nose between his paws. His whiskers hung to the ground and the pain in his heart was terrible.

'What is to become of me?' he cried out aloud. 'My life is over. I am finished. Even the rabbit of death has come to my door. There is nothing left of my life.'

Rahh tumbled to the floor sobbing uncontrollably until he passed into unconsciousness.

25

The White Lands

For days Rahh lay in the burrow; he didn't dare to come out or even look up to the entrance to see if it was light or the dark time. He tried to hide himself beneath the dried grass and huddled up against a wall but there was not even enough to cover him as he shivered in the cold.

Rahh had lain in terror and despair for days but today he knew that he must eat, otherwise he would become too weak to step out of the burrow. He pulled his legs up in front of him and slowly crawled to the entrance.

All was quiet. The wind was not blowing. But as he crept slowly forwards he was aware of becoming colder at each step. Suddenly he was faced with a solid wall where the mouth of the burrow should be; light shone through it yet he couldn't see the other side. Rahh touched the wall with his foot and it was icy cold. What had happened? Had he ended his days? Was this his tomb as the rabbit of death had foretold? Had he passed into the long rabbit sleep?

Rahh pushed at the white wall and it was soft. He put his nose on it and it was wet but also very, very cold – a wall of cold, soft wet stuff like he had never seen before. Although he was weak he began to dig, which is automatic for a rabbit. It's what they like to do.

The white wall gave way easily and soon he had tunnelled out into the open wood. His heart almost stopped: the world had changed. Everything was completely white but also completely still and silent. He looked up at the trees and not a leaf hung upon them. They had become bones, like the rabbit of death who had visited him.

'These must be the white lands of bitterness,' he thought. 'My beautiful world has gone and all that is left is this freezing, dead world of silence. All is death.'

In the burrow he had been sad and frightened but now it was even worse. Nothing lived. All was death and it left a bitter taste in his mouth.

The taste reminded him that he had come out to look for food but there was nothing to eat but the cold, white blanket that was so deep it came up to his nose. It wet his feet and his fur and his heart hurt so much that he cried out loud as tears of unspeakable despair burst from his eyes.

'Golden Rabbit, why have you left me?'

Frozen and broken-hearted, Rahh went back into the burrow. He knew it was his time to enter the long rabbit sleep of no return.

He curled up on the dry grass again, feeling his tears of pain tumble across his paws as his heart burst for Golden Rabbit. For her touch when he was troubled. For her gentle tunes that she offered to the air in the mornings, and for her deep love that he had been wrapped up in for such a long time.

Rahh's little heart pounded with the pain of his loss and he drifted towards the end of his days in the darkness beneath the white lands of bitterness.

26

Reflection

Mother was quiet and the light of the Father had not been seen in the waters of life for a long, long time. The darkness continued to pervade Rahh's miserable existence.

The inner pain of losing his friend had long ago been too much to bear and Rahh had now fallen into surrender and grief. He had let everything go. Now there was nothing between him and the long rabbit sleep, other than the few breaths that still moved his otherwise lifeless body.

He had become weak and semi-conscious. Given up. Hunger no longer bothered him. The darkness in the burrow had actually become cosy in a way. He felt it close to his fur, watching him.

One of his eyes had gone blind as he lay upon his side on the earth. It had been some days since he had opened his useful eye; he was incapable of even that small movement and his thoughts were lost too.

Rahh had left this world. There was no life left in him to think or even to be.

As he entered the next world he became aware of a sensation on his nose. His body tried to jump at the thought that something was trying to eat him. He struggled but did not have the strength to lift himself even though he felt more awake as the strange sensation continued.

A kind of lump became noticeable under Rahh's lip, against his teeth, then there was a kind of pushing as he became aware of a sharp, bitter feeling stinging his mouth. His tongue moved towards it and then he fell back into the space between worlds.

After some time he felt the pushing on his nose again, the

lump under his top lip and the sharpness on his tongue. This process went on for a long time. He would slip away and then be brought back by the pushing on his nose.

Each time it happened he became a little more aware, until one time his eye opened and he saw a small creature in front of him. He became alarmed.

'Is that what is trying to eat me?' he thought. He tried to make a noise to frighten it but he was too weak. The creature had seen Rahh's eye open and it stopped pushing as the two of them stared at each other for a time. When Rahh could no longer keep his eye open, he fell away again.

Day after day the pattern repeated itself: the small creature pushed on Rahh's nose and then Rahh felt the sharp feeling on his tongue. Each day he felt a little more awake until one day he managed to make a small grunt. The creature made a squeak in return and at the sound Rahh realised that it meant him no harm – although he was still confused. In fact, he wasn't really sure what world he was in but he was aware of the little creature running away and returning with something in its mouth.

He dropped it on the floor in front of Rahh's eye so that he could see it. It was a bright red berry. Rahh blinked to show that he understood and then the small creature rolled it towards Rahh's mouth, pushed on his nose to lift his top lip and squeezed the red berry inside. He then bit the berry and the sharp juice squirted onto Rahh's tongue.

Suddenly, energy rushed through Rahh's brain. He knew what was happening. Each day the small creature was feeding him the sharp juice of the berry.

At this realisation a light seemed to come on within him. He felt the beat of his heart and then pain as a small tear came to his eye. A wave of warmth flooded through him as he slipped back into rabbit sleep.

The next time he awoke he was aware that there was new dry grass against his body and he could hear the sounds of other small creatures close by. The ritual continued for many cycles of the Great Light even though Rahh had not seen it, and eventually he was strong enough to move and speak.

'Who are you?' asked Rahh.

'I am Rasp,' the creature replied.

'What are you doing with me?' Rahh said.

'I am putting the water of life onto your tongue from this berry that is full of the juice of life,' explained Rasp.

'I don't understand,' said Rahh.

'You don't understand because you have been very close to the long rabbit sleep and your mind has gone. Your body almost went too, but I found you and I am trying to bring you back into this world,' said Rasp.

Rahh realised that the effort to think and speak was too much, and he dropped his head and closed his eye again.

Rasp called out to some other creatures and they came and pushed the dry grass against Rahh's body to keep him warm. Each night they had all been sleeping next to Rahh to bring the warmth of life back into him.

After some time, Rahh became strong enough to move and lie on his belly. The sight began to return to the eye that had lain in the earth for so long and Rasp brought him nuts and seeds as well as berries to eat. Rahh realised that this was a family of wood mice creatures, whom he had seen from time to time scurrying in the woodland. As Rahh's mind came back to him, he had many questions. One morning he was watching Rasp as he busied himself around the burrow.

'My name is Rahh,' he said.

'Yes, we know who you are,' replied the wood mouse. 'You are the one who was with the shining one until she left the woodland.'

'You know about Golden Rabbit?' asked Rahh, with hope in his voice.

'Yes, we know who she is but we do not know her, and now she has gone and the earth is different. This was her burrow,' said the wood mouse with his whiskers in the air, quite proud that he was sharing the golden one's burrow.

'Yes, everything is different,' said Rahh as his mood dropped and he closed his eyes again. But this time, Rasp came up to Rahh's nose and pulled one of his whiskers. Rahh opened his eyes in surprise and looked at the wood mouse.

Rasp looked Rahh in the eye and said, 'Rahh, it is time for you to awaken. That is why we have come here to help bring you back from the long rabbit sleep. Our time comes for all of us in one life or another, and when we truly embrace it we grow in stature. Mice become men and bunnies become great rabbits. All we have to do is embrace our time with all of our hearts.'

'Now it is time for you to return to life. If it was your time to enter the long rabbit sleep then you would have entered it – but you didn't and so it isn't,' said the wood mouse.

Rahh was quite taken aback by the words of this tiny creature. He spoke with the wisdom of Golden Rabbit, but in a much smaller package.

Rahh said, 'But the white lands of bitterness have killed Mother Earth: all is silent outside the burrow and the trees have turned to bones. I stepped into it and it froze my feet. No rabbits can live in that death.'

'As you wake up, Rahh, you will see the beauty of life reflected to you. Nothing is as it seems but all things are a reflection of what is inside you. If you experienced the cold and bitterness, then that is what you were tasting inside yourself,' said Rasp.

'But there is nothing left inside me since Golden Rabbit went away,' said Rahh.

'So, if there is nothing inside you, then there was nothing inside you before the shining one went away,' said Rasp.

'When Golden Rabbit was here, she only reflected to you what was inside you. Now she has left, whatever was in there remains, Rahh. Soon you will be strong enough to go out of the burrow again, and have a chance to re-enter your world. Then you can see what is inside you by what is reflected to you,' said Rasp.

'But I cannot go out again into the white lands of bitterness. It was too cold for me there,' said Rahh.

'When you are ready you will hear the call of a messenger. The messenger will come and tell you it is time for you to live,' said the wood mouse.

Rahh was becoming tired and the pain in his heart was still great from missing Golden Rabbit now that he was talking about her.

'You must rest again now, Rahh,' said the wood mouse. 'When the messenger comes you will know him by his sign: it will touch you deeply. He will show you a sign of his courage, like a great shield of the warriors of old. Do not worry yourself now but rest and become strong.'

Rahh tried to smile for the first time in a long while. He really appreciated the mouse being there and helping him. He thought for a moment about Zzard and how he too had helped him. Suddenly Rahh realised that many, many beings had been there for him when he needed it – even the cold north wind, which had told him when to go to the burrow.

He closed his eyes and rested.

27

All Things Must Change

Things were changing in the burrow. Rahh could move his feet and stretch his legs. He was now becoming hungry again in the mornings and all the wood mice were bringing him food, whilst Rasp was feeding it to him.

He noticed that he was content in a way, sometimes almost happy. He definitely enjoyed watching the little creatures scurrying about and pushing dry grass against his body to keep him warm. Every now and then they would stop and look at Rahh for a moment as if admiring him in some way and pleased with themselves that they were doing some good and worthwhile work. They seemed to be busy all of the time they were awake.

Some time ago, Rahh had wondered aloud how they could stand the cold outside and Rasp had told him that they had little tunnels in the grass beneath the white lands of bitterness so that the cold was bearable. Although it was cold they could run through these tunnels and find food. Rahh wondered if he would also have to live in tunnels beneath the white lands of bitterness, and where he would find food now that all the green grass had gone.

This morning, all the mice had left the burrow to find food. Rahh was on his own, flexing his growing muscles and twitching his feet. Suddenly he became aware of beautiful music. It touched his heart deeply and made the waters of life flow from his eyes. It also lessened the pain of losing Golden Rabbit a little – or at least he couldn't feel it as much. The music continued to touch him deeply inside and then after a while it stopped.

Rahh lay still listening to his feelings. Something was definitely happening inside him. Something was changing. Perhaps it was because of the food that the wood mice were bringing him.

Shortly the mice returned. Rasp was looking very pleased and joyful this morning.

'Good morning Rahh,' said Rasp, with his whiskers in the air and his nose twitching.

'Good morning, Rasp,' replied Rahh.

'What is the matter, Rahh? I see the waters of life have been pouring down your fur and onto your toes,' Rasp asked.

'Yes, I am not sure what is happening. I heard beautiful music and it touched something inside me and brought the waters of life from my eyes. All kinds of feelings have been stirring inside me since then,' said Rahh.

'But are you alright?' asked Rasp.

'Yes, I think I am fine,' said Rahh, lifting his whiskers and smiling at Rasp.

'I see. Well, I would like you to close your eyes and put out your tongue, for I have a new thing for you to taste this morning.'

'What is it?' Rahh wondered.

'Close your eyes, and see if you like it with your tongue,' said Rasp.

Rahh closed his eyes and Rasp called the wood mice in. They rolled a little package to Rasp and Rasp put it under Rahh's nose and onto his tongue.

Rahh's eyes shot open and the waters of life burst from his eyes again. The wood mice all stood back and watched. Rahh could not speak for a while, until the waters began to stop flowing.

'How is it?' said Rasp.

Rahh said, 'It is a taste from long, long ago, from when I was a tiny bunny, just born and out of the burrow for the first time. It is as if I am reborn again and tasting something for the first time. It fills my tummy with joy and I think even laughter. It does something powerful to my insides that brought the waters of life to my eyes.'

Rasp spoke. 'We found it this morning, pushing through from the mother. It seems very new, just born.'

'Yes,' said Rahh. 'These are the new shoots of the green grass that carry the waters of life into our bodies.' He cried again at the joy he felt from the taste of the new shoots of green grass. He was full of thanks and deep gratitude to the wood mice who had brought this gift for him this morning.

'Yes, we thought this would please you, Rahh. We knew that this is what Golden Rabbit ate in the mornings when she first came to the wood,' said Rasp. 'Now enjoy the taste, whilst we will make ourselves busy with wood mouse work,' and he tootled off with the others in the direction of the entrance to the burrow.

Later that day, Rahh moved his body for the first time and the wood mice tidied his bed where he had lain for such a long, long while.

The following morning the wood mice went out as usual with the promise that they would see if they could find more green shoots. Rahh was sitting up properly for the first time and began to wash his legs and paws.

Suddenly, the beautiful music came down the burrow again and immediately touched Rahh's heart: he felt it expand and fill with joy, and again the waters of life began to flow from his eyes. He took a few steps forward to look towards the entrance of the burrow but could not see any light or where the music was coming from.

He listened to the tuneful sounds until they ceased and then lay down again. It was as if there had been an expansion in his heart. He felt bigger but also exhausted from what it was doing to him. He lay and just listened to what was happening inside him. His feelings seemed to be heightened.

Presently the wood mice returned and Rahh was very keen to see if they had found more new shoots of the fresh green grass. They all wanted to feed Rahh at the same time with what they had discovered and there was quite some excitement in the burrow. The wood mice presented Rahh with the fresh, green shoots and just like before, they had a profound effect on him. Just these few shoots made him feel full and gave strength to his muscles.

Later that evening Rasp wandered over to Rahh. Rahh watched him coming and propped himself up on his front paws.

Rasp spoke: 'Rahh, do you recall that I told you that a messenger would come for you?'

'Yes,' said Rahh.

'And do you recall that I said that you would know him by his sign?'

'Yes, I remember that too, Rasp,' said Rahh.

Rasp continued. 'Today when we returned from gathering foods from the forest, I could see that the waters of life had again been running from your eyes. Did you hear the beautiful music again?'

'Yes, I heard it again; and as you saw it brought the waters of life to my eyes once more. But also, this time, I felt it deeply in my heart. I knew that I was becoming stronger. I also felt fear – fear about going back into the world outside the burrow. I have been in this dark place for a long, long time beneath the white lands of bitterness. My life almost left me and I am still not sure if that would not have been the best thing. But then, when the green shoots touched my tongue, there was such a rush of life into my body that it wanted to burst out of the burrow. And memories of Golden Rabbit came back too as we spent so much time together eating the green shoots and laughing.'

Rasp spoke again. 'Yesterday, I had a feeling your messenger had come for you; and today I am certain of it. The music is preparing you to re-enter your life and your mission in this world.'

'But what is the sign?' asked Rahh.

'The sign is the way the light in the music opens your heart, Rahh, and in turn makes the waters of life flow. Whenever the heart is touched by beauty and love, it has no choice other than to open like a flower seeking the Great Light in the blue, and then the waters of life will always flow. As the waters of life flow, they take the pain from your broken body a little at a time,' said Rasp.

Rahh, of course, had heard this great wisdom from Golden Rabbit. Now this small wood mouse also seemed to be full of the same knowledge, as he had once thought before.

Rahh spoke. 'How do you know such things, Rasp? Whenever you speak it is as if you have the wisdom of the Heavens upon your words and you speak the same wisdom as Golden Rabbit.'

'We are of the same sign,' said Rasp. 'We have learned the ways of the wood and how to walk our path through the wood by living with an open heart. So, even though I did not know Golden Rabbit, I could see her sign and she could see mine. We are the same.'

'But you are a wood mouse, and she was a rabbit,' said Rahh.

'That is so, but we are the same inside. Our hearts have grown and become free because we had the courage to leave the others and follow a different path. We did not listen to the things that others told us were right and proper, but we listened to the feelings in our hearts and followed those. Those feelings led us into a great and expanded world. The Mother and the Father opened things for us to see and feel, like you felt the music this past two mornings. Your heart is hearing in a new way. A way it has not heard before. The music has always been there, Rahh, but you have been unable to hear it due to rabbit thoughts limiting your growth.'

Rahh felt the wisdom and realised how small he was compared with this wood mouse. Rasp watched Rahh as the waters of life came from his deep brown eyes again.

Rasp continued.

'When the heart grows it is painful. It opens like the petals of a flower. Each petal is painful, but once open it can never close again. As these petals open you feel more joy in life but you can also feel more pain too,' said Rasp.

'This is because your heart is given to you for each life you are born into. In some lives it is a dark heart full of malice, greed and hatred, and all forms of dark feelings. The heart is too frightened to grow and blossom and so it lives a life which is governed by fear. The creature that is governed by a heart full of fear is capable of some very dark deeds, for it has no compassion and understanding of the lives and the pain of others,' said Rasp.

'Rahh, the music you are hearing has always been there. Each morning it sings out as the Great Light rises into the blue; sometimes your ears may have heard it, but now your heart hears it too. This is the sign that you are growing. You feel the love, the light and the joy in the music as it opens your petals. To show you this growth, a messenger has been sent for you. The green shoots have been sent and your strength is returning. You must prepare yourself, Rahh. It is time for you to leave the burrow and walk upon the Mother again. You will see there have been changes, for all things grow and change. Even entering the long rabbit sleep is growing into change. This time though, it was not your time to sleep but to re-awaken,' said Rasp.

'Now you must rest again, Rahh,' Rasp went on. 'If the music comes a third time, it will be announcing the rising of the Great Light into the blue. You may find that your body lifts itself in preparation to breathe the outside air once more, and then you will be ready to walk in the ways of the wise ones again, taking your place in the world and bringing your light into the wood. I will sleep next to you for comfort,' said Rasp.

Rasp curled up next to Rahh and Rahh indeed felt the comfort of another beating heart full of love beside him.

'Good night, Rahh.'

'Good night Rasp and thank you,' said Rahh.

28

The Messenger

Rahh was waking from a deep dream of rabbit heaven. He could taste the green shoots on his tongue as he awoke. Rasp was already up and out in the world and so were the other wood mice.

'Did Rasp really speak all those words of wisdom like Golden Rabbit, last night, or was it a dream?' Rahh wondered.

Suddenly, he realised that he had been dreaming of the fresh green shoots because he could smell them. He opened his eyes, and there in front of him just a few paces away, was a full feast of breakfast shoots waiting for him. Before Rahh knew what was happening, his body had moved by itself and he was up and nibbling. The fresh waters of life graced his tongue and joy filled his heart and tummy.

He finished his meal and was thinking that this was almost like eating a Light breakfast with Golden Rabbit, when suddenly the beautiful music came down the burrow again.

Rahh felt the lion in his heart for the first time since the great Zzard had bid him good morning such a long time ago. It was different this time: he felt that the lion had a different quality – not ready for battle but ready with determination. The determination to find out where the music was coming from. Even without thinking the lion in him brought strength to his limbs and he began to hop up the tunnel of the burrow towards the surface.

He saw a brightly lit world just beyond the entrance. It touched his eyes and as they squinted and focused he could see that there was a black shape at the entrance to the burrow blocking his way.

The music continued to fall into his rabbit ears when he heard the lion in him speak.

'Stand back from my house. You are blocking the light and I must find out the source of this beautiful music,' said Rahh.

The dark shape fluttered, flapped and jumped.

'Ah, so, foolish rabbit,' said a squeaky little voice. 'You think you can frighten me out of the way with your inner lion. You are not even quick enough to catch a breath, let alone catch me,' said the shape, laughing at Rahh.

Rahh's lion came up even stronger.

'You are standing in the way of my light,' he roared in a strong voice that shook his whiskers.

The shape just laughed and then began to hop and dance in front of Rahh.

'You are looking for your light in the wrong place. It is not outside you, it is inside, you hopping gerbil,' it mocked.

Rahh felt the sting of this 'gerbil' insult. It caused him a great pain inside and the creature's laughter made things worse. He thought to himself, 'If I was stronger I would give him the rabbit kick; then we'd see how he laughed.'

Suddenly the shape became smaller and more light flooded down the burrow. It was so bright that Rahh could hardly stand it. He felt trapped and was just about to rush for the entrance when the beautiful music came again. It touched Rahh's heart and his lion melted away. Then the shape was gone and the bright light of the white lands of bitterness filled his sight. Slowly, he walked to the entrance with his eyes almost closed against the brightness: he had been down in the dark burrow for so long it seemed impossible to open his eyes fully. At last he felt that he was stepping out of the darkness and into the light once more.

Rahh poked his nose out of the burrow and sniffed the fresh air. It lifted his heart and he realised how different it was from the air in the burrow, which was tainted with the smell of a rabbit who had tried to enter the long rabbit sleep.

He couldn't see the shape any longer but he could still hear the music. As his eyes became used to the light he began to look around. The brightness was intense but he soon realised that he could not feel the freezing cold of the white lands of bitterness. He looked at his paws and saw the new shoots of green grass upon the earth. He recognised the little glade outside the burrow, just as it had been before the white lands of bitterness arrived.

'Am I going mad?' he thought. 'Has it been like this all the time but I could not see it?'

Rahh was suddenly confused as rabbits sometimes can be. There was too much happening again as soon as he had stepped out of the safety of the burrow. A laughing, flapping shape calling him a gerbil was painful, but the beautiful music and a belly full of green juice was glorious. And now all this brightness but no cold or white lands of bitterness any more. The Mother had changed her cloak since last he trod upon her earth.

'I see your thoughts, gerbil,' said a twittering voice. 'How does the bitterness and the cold feel now? Is it all gone or do you feel that there is more inside you?'

Rahh's eyes had adjusted to the intense light. He looked around and still could not see where the voice was coming from. In fact, it seemed to be coming from different places each time it spoke.

'Prick up your ears, rabbit,' it said. 'Have you forgotten how to know where things are?'

'Sometimes they are distant,
Sometimes they are close,
Sometimes beneath you
Or as high as a rose,'
sang the voice.

Rahh pricked up his ears and turned them this way and that, but could not find the source of the twitterer.

'Show yourself you twittering shadow,' he shouted, with a

touch of rabbit lion in his voice, but it was not as powerful as the proper lion that usually came out of his heart. 'Why do you mock me? I have done nothing to you.'

'What you do to yourself you do to all creatures,' said the voice. 'If you try to put yourself into the long rabbit sleep then you wish the same upon others, even though you don't know the power of your own thoughts,' it continued.

'What nonsense is this?' thought Rahh.

'It is not nonsense,' the voice said. 'I told you that I could hear your thoughts.'

'Now I can't even think without being watched, mocked or laughed at by this demon,' Rahh fumed.

'That's right,' the voice laughed. 'Now listen whilst I tell you daft rabbit, that there are many things you don't know and even more that you would not like to know; but all of them you will know, sooner or later. The later you leave it the more work you will have to do to catch up. Now I will tell you a story.'

'Once there was a Great Light that came to the Mother and she gave birth to all things that you see. All things that move. All things that grow and all things that you eat. She gave birth to you, rabbit. You came from your Mother and Father, but before that, you came from your greater Mother and Father. Without them forming their union, which shines upon you each day, you would be nothing but nothing, not even a single thing,' the voice said.

'You have experienced death down in the burrow. You have experienced the darkness of losing the light that feeds you; and you have experienced the darkness and pain of the white lands of bitterness. That pain is nothing but a part of the journey that is suffered by all creatures who receive the gift of the light.'

'Now you have come from your Mother's womb once more and into the light of the world, feeling again the warmth of the Great Light upon your fur.'

'Behind all pain is love, and behind love is light; and all

animals must fight a great battle within themselves to find that light. When they find it they will shine like the Great Light in the blue,' continued the voice.

'So, jumping rabbit. Are you going to continue jumping in circles all your life or are you going to begin to truly live from the light that shines within you?'

Rahh was not sure if he should answer. He was not sure if the twittering voice had finished. Whilst he was still contemplating all these words – too many for such an early time of day – the twitterer stood in front of him, tiny by comparison to himself, but yet so full of words.

It hopped like a rabbit but had feathers like the great Zzard, and on its breast it had a great red shield. It opened its beak and the most beautiful music came out of it. Rahh stepped back in amazement not knowing what to do or say.

'Do nothing, say nothing,' said the creature, reading Rahh's thoughts.

'Don't listen to my song of joy that bursts your heart open but *hear* it. Creatures listen to many things, but they don't often hear the truth in the message. When you can hear with your heart then you will truly live,' said the creature.

Rahh knew that this was his messenger but that didn't make him feel very comfortable: he realised that he might be in for another difficult time of trying to understand new things. He thought perhaps that he should run back down the burrow and continue to be fed by the wood mice.

'The wood mice have left,' said the creature, reading Rahh's thoughts again.

'Have you frightened them away?' said Rahh, with alarm in his voice.

'No, their work is done. It is finished. They did what they came to do and now the world is changing and they have other things to do and other places to be,' replied the red-breasted twitterer.

'But I love them,' said Rahh, surprised by his own words as

he had not previously thought about loving the tiny creatures. 'I love them, and now you say they have gone!'

Rahh felt the pain in his heart again of losing friends that he loved. This life was so difficult, and always just as things seemed to be getting better they got worse again.

'Small rabbit,' said the creature – but Rahh jumped in and interrupted him.

'I am bigger than you are,' he said, with a rush of anger in his voice.

'Small rabbit, you might be big in the body but you are small in the experiences of walking through the forest of life,' it replied. 'I will guide you for part of the way if you wish it. As you see, all is now changed upon the face of our Mother and the green shoots grow again ready to receive you; to feed you; to nurture you. These things nurture your body but the experiences of the forest path nurture your inner light,' said the creature.

'As you see the white lands of bitterness have given way to a new birth of all things that grow. The power of love is again bursting forth from the breasts of the Mother. You have felt my music touch you deeply in the heart and so you know who I am. Tonight you will lay in your burrow alone rabbit, and tomorrow I will sing my song for the last time at your door. Then you will choose if you are ready to emerge into light or if you will stay in the darkness that you have created for yourself down below.'

The creature opened its wings and hopped and Rahh saw the great red shield on its breast flash before him as if filled with light. The music and the red shield: two signs that this must be the messenger who had come for him.

'Who are you?' asked Rahh. 'How do I know that I should walk with you? How do I know that it is safe for me?'

'I am Fuff, a Guardian and Guide. I lift the spirits of all those who can hear. I show the way to all those who can see. I am small, but big. I am light as a feather and so I dance in the morning air as I sing out to those who wish to receive joy into their hearts.

I am the carrier of news from one part of the wood to another and I rest in the branches in the dark time where I can hear every breath of every creature as they sleep, and even those that roam the woods in the dark, like the striped heads.'

'If you walk in my way you will not know if it is safe or if you are going the right way until you feel the truth in your heart. In order to feel the truth, then you must take a chance and trust if it feels right. If it feels right; if it feels exciting; or if it feels like it is your next step.'

'I am the messenger of the dawn. My voice brings forth the Great Light in the blue and lays to rest the dark time. I am Fuff, the minstrel of life.'

'For all those with ears, let them hear; and for all those with eyes, then let them see, for I will show them the way.'

'Tomorrow, rabbit, I will stand at the door of your heart and bathe it in love with the music that you can hear. You will have but a moment of time to choose whether to follow this music or not, for then I will be gone upon the changing wind.'

'Farewell my rabbit friend, until the next rising of the Great Light.'

The feathered creature looked deeply into Rahh's eyes, flapped his wings once and took to the air at great speed, leaving Rahh with much thinking to do.

29

Pause for Thought

The Great Light was rising into the blue and Rahh sat by the entrance to the burrow, looking up and wondering where the creature had gone. It had merely flapped its wings and disappeared in a red and brown blur.

As he sat, he could feel the warmth of the brightening day on his fur. It had been such a long time since he felt such warmth. He began to look around and could see new shoots of grass everywhere; there was no sign of the white lands of bitterness – only a fresh green glow. He wondered once more if he had spent a long time dreaming in the burrow. And what about the wood mice? Where had they gone and why did they not say goodbye?

Rahh was as confused as a rabbit could be. He had come out of the darkness of his burrow and his friends who had kept him alive and fed him had gone without a word. Now this Fuff creature had arrived, calling him names like *daft rabbit* and *hopping gerbil* and what was worse it could also see his thoughts. Suddenly, he felt his tummy calling to the green shoots and he hopped into the air in a kind of automatic response to some stimulus, which took him by surprise.

'It must be the smell of the new green shoots,' he thought.

Rahh turned around and looked in all directions. He was most definitely alone and it seemed safe, so he thought that he might just sit in the warmth of the morning and nibble. He was feeling rather pleased with himself although he had no idea why. There was joy in his mood and his fur bristled outwards towards the blue. He brushed his whiskers with his paws and settled down to taste fresh, green breakfast grass.

Rahh ate the most wonderful breakfast. It seemed very special to him this day. It was as if everything was new and the feeling of the waters of life in the green juice were filling him with happiness. He didn't really seem to be too sad that the wood mice had left but at the same time he was hopeful that they would return. 'I really did like them,' he thought to himself. It was very comforting to know that they were in the burrow with him, living in their own little way in a corner, but popping out now and then to look at him. He definitely didn't feel lonely when they were near.

'Yes, these are good thoughts and this is a good day and these new shoots are very good too,' thought Rahh, as he lay down on his belly and began to doze in a ray of sunlight that was finding its way through the tall trees around his burrow.

Rahh was still weak and very tired from his close brush with the long rabbit sleep. It would take time for him to fully recover but for now he was happy. As the day rolled forward, the Great Light in the blue passed over the heaven point and began to fall back towards the Mother. Rahh felt the movement of the Great Light and it woke him as if to say goodnight.

A slight evening breeze stirred the woodland floor and Rahh shivered. He lifted his ears and bristled his whiskers upwards. Even just making these two movements was exciting to him, as he had been in stillness and darkness for so long. Just feeling his paw on the new shoots was good and he found himself saying 'thank you', although he had no idea who to.

He wanted to stay out and watch the blue turn dark but it was getting cold and he knew that he must go under the earth again for warmth and safety. He gave himself the pleasure of watching the Great Light turning yellow before it went beneath the Mother, and then he stood up, stretched his legs and popped down the burrow.

30

Great Thoughts

There was a warmth in the burrow even though only he and the wood mice had inhabited it for quite some time. Rahh could feel the place was lived in since going outside and sensed the energies of the growing cycle of light.

Rahh was quite happy with himself even though his first day out of the burrow had been challenging in some ways – not least because he didn't have the energy to do very much. He felt that a few short steps outside had done him some good though: he most definitely felt better.

He scurried about the burrow and made himself a new bed, using the soft material that the wood mice had left in their little corner. He turned around and settled on the spot where he had lain for such a long, long time. Where the wood mice had fed him and where he had also felt the deep pain of losing Golden Rabbit.

Rahh put his nose between his paws and his chin on the earth. Although he was happy, he was also aware of a deep sadness and uncertainty within him. He must beware not to fall into it, he thought.

He remembered that this was Golden Rabbit's burrow and he wondered if that was why he could feel warmth again here now. Then his mind drifted to the wonderful smell of the new shoots of grass that the wood mice brought to him only this morning, and already it seemed like a lifetime away.

A word came into his mind. 'Kindness.'

Yes, he thought. The wood mice had been so kind to him. In fact, if they had not pushed food into his mouth he would certainly have entered the long rabbit sleep and never seen another green shoot of grass. He had a sudden feeling of horror that he could have lost his life and realised that he had indeed been a very 'daft rabbit', as Fuff had put it.

Rahh began to drift into a gentle sleep. He realised as he slipped away that he was loved but at the same time he didn't know who by, as all his friends had gone. But the feeling of being loved carried him into the dream time.

Soon enough, the dark time was over and he felt his whiskers bristling upwards and his back legs stretching out by themselves. His body was remembering what a rabbit was and how it should function, whilst his head was still partly in the world of sleep.

Rahh suddenly shot awake, remembering what was to happen today. He was to listen out for the music, which would only sound once more and then be gone and he wondered if he had slept through it. In his alarm his legs sprang forward and carried him up to the mouth of the burrow. He poked his head out and looked around. All was quiet but there was pale light in the blue and he realised that it was still early: hopefully the Messenger of the Dawn had not already been and called the Great Light into the blue from beneath the cloak of Mother.

Rahh sat for a moment gathering himself together and noticed the green shoots in the glade nearby. As he thought about having a nibble, the music began to call. Rahh's ears stood up and he felt his heart fill with joy. What was this music, and how did it do this to him, he wondered. At the same time he was captivated by the feelings of love that seemed to wash through him each time he heard it. He felt loved, as he did last night in the burrow.

Suddenly, Fuff was standing in front of him, the air fizzing with his movement.

'Have you said goodbye to your bed and your burrow?' asked Fuff.

'Goodbye?' said Rahh, somewhat alarmed.

'Yes. Goodbye. You will not be coming back here again if you follow me this morning,' Fuff replied.

Rahh's mouth fell open but no words came. Many thoughts

rushed through his furry head but one in particular stood out: 'I am only just out of the burrow again and already there is a great challenge!'

'But last night as I was going to bed, I felt loved in the burrow. I don't think I want to leave that feeling behind. It was warm and comforting and I felt safe,' he said.

'What kind of rabbit are you?' asked Fuff, with irritation in his voice. 'Are you a rabbit rabbit or a Golden Rabbit?'

'Well, I am just an ordinary rabbit,' Rahh replied.

'But I was guided to your burrow and the greatest light beyond the Great Light told me that I would find a Golden Rabbit here,' said Fuff in his sharp way of speaking.

'Well, that is true, but you have missed the Golden Rabbit. She left some time before the white lands of bitterness came. I moved into the burrow when she had gone,' said Rahh.

Fuff flapped and whistled into a red and brown blur and shot up into the blue. He moved so quickly that Rahh could not see where he had gone. Then his twittering voice called out from above.

'So you tricked me. You are a tricksy rabbit. All this time you were an impostor in the Golden Rabbit's burrow, pretending to be golden,' he shrieked, quite angry now.

Rahh looked upwards in the direction of the twittering and shouted back. 'I did not trick anyone. I am just me and I was living in the burrow of my friend, hoping that she might come back and find me there. I did not pretend to be anyone else. I was just me!'

'Well, what am I going to do now? I have been misled,' shot back Fuff. 'I am supposed to find a Golden Rabbit here and teach him the mysteries of Mother. Where has the Golden Rabbit gone? Perhaps I need to follow after him and find him.'

'Golden Rabbit is a she. We think that she was taken for food by the pack creatures. There has been no sign of her since before the time of the white lands of bitterness,' explained Rahh.

Fuff whistled loudly and the red and brown blur suddenly arrived on the ground in front of Rahh again.

'So long ago! She went even before the white lands of bitterness,' Fuff repeated, shaking his head as he looked at the earth.

Rahh could see that the creature was struggling with the situation and suggested that perhaps Fuff might like to take some breakfast with him; maybe some answers would come.

'Breakfast! Breakfast!' shouted Fuff, animated again and spinning around at least a hundred times. 'I had my breakfast as I was calling the Great Light into the blue, whilst you were still sleeping your life away, ordinary rabbit,' he barked in annoyance.

At this stinging insult, Rahh said, 'Well, I think I am more than ready for a few green shoots of breakfast grass, and you can come with me or stay here looking like a moth-eaten ball of moss.'

Rahh was surprised at his courage returning and his whiskers bristled with life as he looked at this perplexing and perplexed feathered creature. 'I shall go to the Field of Wonders and see how the shoots are coming along,' he decided.

Rahh turned and without looking back began to retrace his memory of the path through the wood to where the Field of Wonders lay. It wasn't long before he stood at the fence. He kissed Mother Earth and asked for her permission to enter. He said a little prayer to give thanks for bringing him here safely. He didn't look back once to see was the flapping creature following him. His eye and his heart were set on eating a Light breakfast for the first time in a very long time.

Rahh stepped into the Field of Wonders and looked around. Everything was new but he recognised the place. He made a path through the wet morning grass to where he and Golden Rabbit had spent many hours bathing in the sun and discussing great stories about life. The little bush was there where they took shade when the Great Light was too hot, and there was even a little indentation in the ground where they had rolled on their backs to walk with their feet in the blue.

Rahh focused his vision carefully upon a single drop of the water of life. He became very still and allowed his heart to feel into the truth of the drop of water. Yes, there was a stingingly bright red jewel, the light of which pierced Rahh's heart the second that he saw it.

Then a stunning green jewel and a yellow jewel. He took them one by one onto his tongue and gave thanks. Today all the colours were here and he took each one into his mouth with a fine, fresh blade of green juicy grass as an accompaniment.

'What a divine breakfast of Light,' thought Rahh. He began to feel alive and again that he was loved. He was just fine on his own and he didn't need this noisy twittering irritation that called itself a guide. He could guide himself with the help of a Light breakfast each morning.

Then suddenly the thought became bigger. He really felt it in his heart and repeated it aloud. 'I don't need anybody. I am just fine on my own. I feel loved by Mother and Father and I feel like I know where I am going.'

Then another great thought came into his head and he felt overwhelmed with the energy of it. Suddenly he was tired and had to lie down to think it properly.

'If I don't need anybody then I can be with anybody. I am self-sufficient within myself and so I can choose who to be with or to be on my own. I am so very happy with knowing this deep inside me,' thought Rahh.

As he lay pondering these great thoughts and what they meant, a sudden whirlwind of brown and red arrived on top of the bush next to him. Fuff looked down at Rahh and Rahh looked up at Fuff. They continued to look at each other for quite a while and neither spoke.

Then Fuff hummed a sweet tune – not like the beautiful music of the morning but very sweet and gentle. It was a tune full of lilting love. Rahh lifted his ears to listen and then to hear it in his heart.

Rahh felt the love inside Fuff coming out through his music, even though this creature was full of vile antagonisms. He was most definitely a bag of contradictions, thought Rahh.

Once Fuff had stopped singing he looked down at Rahh. Rahh's lion was coming up: he could feel it – not too strongly, but strongly enough to say what he wanted to say.

'That was very lovely music, Fuff. I will miss it now that you will not be my guardian and guide.'

'Well, what do you mean?' asked Fuff.

'I am quite happy on my own and I don't need to go with you. I am not the Golden Rabbit that you were looking for and so you may go your own way,' said Rahh.

'But I have instructions,' replied Fuff. 'I was told by the light beyond all lights that I was to guide the rabbit that came out of the burrow.'

'But I am not the rabbit you thought, Fuff. My burrow is a short distance away and I was only staying temporarily in the burrow of Golden Rabbit. You have arrived too late and have also made a mistake,' said Rahh.

'But all the other signs were there,' Fuff pondered. 'The wood mice, the new green shoots of grass, the warming of the Great Light in the blue and a sickly rabbit – namely you,' Fuff pointed at Rahh with his beak.

'All the things I was led to expect and so the timing is correct, but it seems that the Golden Rabbit made an error of judgement and has been eaten. So what shall I do now?' asked Fuff in a voice that was suddenly lost and empty. He was suddenly not as brash and important as he had thought only yesterday and this morning.

Then Rahh had another great thought. This was turning out to be an interesting morning, with so many great thoughts, he thought ... becoming a little confused about thinking about his thoughts. He took a deep breath and said, 'Perhaps I have an idea.'

'What is that?' asked Fuff.

'What were you supposed to do with Golden Rabbit?'

'I was supposed to take her into the deepest part of the forest and share with her some of the mysteries of Mother Earth,' said Fuff.

'Is this a place you have been before?' asked Rahh.

'I have been in many deep forests for the woods and the forests are my domain. I have created my music at the tops of trees in the dawn and the dusk in a great many places,' said Fuff proudly.

'Well, perhaps we might go together,' said Rahh. 'Perhaps you can show me some of these mysteries instead. I have never been into the deep forest.'

Fuff thought for a moment and then said, 'Well, I don't know. I had very clear instructions and you were not a part of them. I could end up going off my path and in the wrong direction if I go wandering off with you, rabbit. And anyway, you are a sickly rabbit. You may enter the long rabbit sleep at any time,' said Fuff, not quite unkindly but speaking his thoughts.

Then he fluttered down gently and stood in front of Rahh.

'What do you think, rabbit?' he said, a little stuck for his own answers.

'I think that I have come out into the world again from a very dark place and I am ready to learn new things. If you have new things to show me then perhaps we might travel together for a while and see how the journey unfolds,' said Rahh.

'If we go forward together perhaps we can find a new woodland to begin the journey in, and if you are given new instructions then we can face those at that time. In the meantime you do not have any instructions to follow, so for the time being you are free of your service,' said Rahh, quite pleased with this little speech.

Fuff spun around, flapped and hopped up and down. This seemed like some kind of thinking process, thought Rahh.

[134]

'That is an interesting thought, rabbit. Yes, we can try that. It feels like a good plan. How shall we proceed?'

Indeed, there were many new and interesting thoughts coming up this morning. Fuff spun into his whirlwind self of blurred red and brown and manifested at the top of the bush in a flash. He looked around in all directions and began to create his music again, giving Rahh time to contemplate.

Rahh lay on the grass warming his fur and hearing the music deep inside his heart whilst thinking.

'This could be an interesting adventure and I think that I have just left my home again. I feel that it is not a good idea to go back but to go forward. The past is the past and I have walked out of it this morning and filled my belly with a Light breakfast, so I am ready.'

'And this fluttering creature seems to fill my heart with love, through its music.'

'Yes, I think everything feels right to proceed,' thought Rahh.

31

Into the East

The day was drawing on. Rahh had lay and rested for a good long time, allowing his Light breakfast to nurture his weakened body, along with the Great Light in the blue filling him with warmth. But he was becoming restless. He felt that it was time to be moving.

Fuff had been singing his song for what seemed like an age, but never grew wearisome. As Rahh began to stir from his rest, he looked up at the brown and red creature and felt love in his heart. 'Yes,' he thought to himself. 'This will be a lovely journey together.'

'Fuff,' shouted Rahh, to cut through the never-ending musical phrases that filled the air with joy. 'It is time we made a plan of where we are going. Do you know the way?'

Fuff suddenly disappeared in a pink flurry and appeared on the ground in front of Rahh. Looking up at the rabbit he said, 'We should enter the woodland in that direction,' pointing with his beak.

'It is the east and all journeys begin walking into the east – for that is where our future lies. We must walk in the direction that the Great Light rises into the blue to meet us and it will show us the way,' said Fuff.

'Then let us go before the dark time comes, or we will not be able to see where we are going,' said Rahh.

'Wait,' said Fuff.

'First I must apologise for I do not know how you are called.'

'My name is Rahh.'

'Bless you Rahh. Now we are ready to begin,' said Fuff.

'Indeed, let us begin,' he replied.

[136]

Fuff took to the air and flew ahead and Rahh followed him towards the edge of the wood. Fuff alighted on the top of a fence post, waiting. Rahh soon caught up and was feeling warm from the movement of his body.

'I must wait here for a moment,' said Rahh.

'What are you waiting for?'

'I need a moment to say goodbye to my old life and the things that I loved,' Rahh replied.

'But you may be coming back this way again soon,' said Fuff.

'No,' said Rahh. 'If I pass this way again, I will be a different me. The old me stays here with the memories of all that I was when I crossed this fence line with you, Fuff. All will now be new and I cannot take the old with me, for it is heavy and burdensome,' said Rahh.

'You are a wise rabbit Rahh,' said Fuff. 'I must listen to your wisdom often.'

Rahh did not really think about feeling good about Fuff's compliments but felt that it was important to acknowledge all things that had past and then let them go. Fuff sat on his post waiting patiently for what Rahh had to do.

Rahh looked into the field and spoke aloud. 'Dearest Field of Wonders. Thank you for all the times you have nurtured me whilst I was walking by the side of Golden Rabbit. Thank you.'

'Dearest Great Light in the blue. Thank you for all the times that you brought warmth into my body when I lay beneath you with Golden Rabbit. Thank you.'

'Dearest bright jewels of the Earth Mother. Thank you for all the light that you brought into my life through this great gift of seeing, taught to me by Golden Rabbit. Thank you.'

'Dearest friends that I have walked with on my journey through life, Zzard and the wood mice. Thank you for being there when I needed help. Thank you.'

'Dearest Golden Rabbit, wherever you now walk, I send my love to you. Thank you.'

Rahh bent his head to the ground and took a single blade

of grass into his mouth slowly, then said, 'I eat this last blade of good sweet grass from you, Field of Wonders, in remembrance of all the wonderful things that have happened to me on this journey since I left my family. I will remember the taste of this sweetness of life that I have been blessed with.'

Rahh turned and popped under the fence, leaving the Field of Wonders behind him. He looked up at Fuff and said simply, 'I am ready.'

'Thank you for sharing your words,' said Fuff. 'I could feel great love in them.'

'Thank you,' said Rahh. 'Now I think we must move on and find a place for our first night together.'

Fuff then entered the woodland and Rahh took his first step into his new future. Looking ahead he could see Fuff waiting for him bobbing up and down on the branch of a tree. Rahh took a huge leap and bounded into the wood, and Fuff took flight, guiding the rabbit to who knows where.

32

The First Night

Fuff would fly ahead and scout the way. Rahh would follow at his rabbit pace and the two creatures soon found a rhythm that was very much in the flow with each other. Of course, Fuff was much quicker and fleet of wing but Rahh was solid on the ground, listening to the heartbeat of Mother, whilst Fuff was in the air of Father. As a team, they brought Heaven and Earth together, each with their own particular gifts.

Fuff flew down and stood on the path waiting for Rahh. As Rahh arrived, Fuff said. 'It is time for us to find a place to sleep, Rahh, but there is no burrow here.'

'It's alright Fuff, I shall find shelter and will be fine, if not as warm and dry as usual. Let us look around for a place to rest. But what about you, how do you sleep?' asked Rahh.

'I also burrow,' he replied. 'I burrow deep into the tightly closed branches of a bush and beneath some draping leaves and I can sleep in a new place every time the dark time comes, because I need no particular fixed home. I can fly free and rest easily anywhere that I find myself.'

Rahh thought this was a very wonderful way to be able to live, and he looked forward to learning more.

'Very well. Will you find a place that suits you? Then I will rest beneath you on the ground, below the safety of your safe place.'

'I will,' said Fuff, and flew upwards and behind some tall trees. When he found his place for the night he began to sing his evening song and Rahh followed the sound. As Rahh arrived, Fuff flew down to meet him.

'I will sleep in this bush,' he said. 'There are some soft leaves beneath it from the end of the last season of warmth. Perhaps you can cover yourself with those, Rahh?'

Rahh squeezed under the bush and said, 'Yes, this is a fine place. It feels very cosy and the winds of the dark time will not be able come close to me here.' He scratched at the ground and made a small hollow to lie in then pulled up some leaves around himself.

Fuff also picked up a few leaves with his beak and tossed them behind Rahh, helping to make him more comfortable. Rahh thanked the feathered creature and said that he felt very happy here in this new home.

Fuff was pleased that they were getting along and then said to Rahh, I must now fly to the top of the trees to sing until the last glimmer of light leaves the blue. My song is to give thanks to the Great Light in the blue for all the work he has done for us today. It is my job also to ask him to rise from his slumbers again soon, so that we may have light. In this way I honour the Great Light in the blue so that all creatures on the Mother may have light in their lives at the next rising. It is my most important work in helping to keep all things living,' said Fuff.

'That is very interesting Fuff,' said Rahh. 'I can feel the love in your song and I am sure the Great Light in the blue is very thankful each day that you have taken some of your valuable time to give thanks and also to welcome him on the following morning. He must surely feel loved by the work that you offer.'

Fuff then burst into a flurry of red and brown feathers and was gone in a flash. Rahh listened as Fuff sang and before he knew it he was asleep.

33

The Invisibility

Rahh awoke to the sound of the sweetest music he had ever heard. It was the same melody that had enticed him from Golden Rabbit's old burrow but somehow different this morning.

He stretched his legs and sniffed at the earth. It was a strange experience sleeping outside a burrow. He felt the morning waking as the Great Light in the blue pushed back the dark time. Normally the Great Light was already some way into the blue by the time he came out of his burrow.

Rahh poked his head out from under the bush where he had slept and then came out into the world. He looked up to see where Fuff was making his music and then around to see if there were any green, juicy blades to eat for breakfast.

Fuff became aware of Rahh's movements and after a short while descended in a flash of brown and red.

'How did you sleep, Rahh?' he asked.

'I slept very well, thank you, and dreamed a peaceful dream of flowers in the meadow – the yellow flower called Lion,' said Rahh.

'That is a good sign, Rahh. When you dream about the Dandelion flower it means that you are in good company and will have a happy union with your chosen friend or partner. It also represents good luck and is like the Great Light in the blue, which radiates your love and thoughts and affections to all those whom you love,' Fuff explained.

'That's a lot of words about a flower, Fuff,' said Rahh. 'Indeed, the dream was very wonderful and full of peace.'

'You can eat the Lion flower for breakfast, Rahh, but it is not time for them yet. They will come soon as the Great Light climbs higher and stays longer in the blue. First the buds of the healers need to swell and ripen; that time is already with us,' Fuff said.

'What are buds and healers?' asked Rahh.

'I can live in different worlds from you, Rahh,' said Fuff. 'I can be on the Mother Earth here, or I can live in the arms of the Healers, perched high up where the winds of change blow. I can even go higher than that and rise completely into the blue and then float down again, but you are stuck on the ground Rahh, because you are different. We are all different.'

'To answer your question, the Healers are the bridge between Heaven and Earth. They are these great, tall beings with roots that go down deep into the earth and arms that reach up towards Heaven. Sometimes rabbits make their burrow between their toes. If you listen carefully to the music of the morning, it comes from creatures that live upon the fingers of these great, tall beings. We call them healers, for that is what they are. When we are sick we go to the healers and sit with them, and they look into us in a gentle way and take away the darkness that causes our unease.'

Fuff continued, 'Also, some creatures make a great deal of smoke and filth that fills the air that we breathe and the healers help to cleanse this.'

Rahh was fascinated to hear about this great new world and how it worked. He sat looking at Fuff, who was bobbing up and down and hopping hither and thither as he spoke.

'Are you with me so far, Rahh?' asked Fuff.

'Oh, yes,' Rahh replied, his mind creating wonderful pictures and images around Fuff's words.

'And then you asked what buds are,' said Fuff. 'Buds are known as the Children of the Forest. There are a great number, more than any rabbit could count in a single wood. It would be very difficult to count them all even if you were the best counting rabbit upon the earth. At this time in the great cycle of light you see them every day in huge numbers.'

'When the great cycle of light shortens and the cold winds come then the healers call to the wind spirit to strip them of their cloaks of summer. Their cloak turns from radiant green to reds, golds and browns and then the wind spirit helps the healers to lay their rich colours upon the earth. Last night, Rahh, you made yourself comfortable with the threads of last season's cloak. You call them leaves. Some say that they come and they go but really they are born of the buds and they leave once they are exhausted,' said Fuff.

'When the healers are ready to give their leaves to sister wind, in those shorter, cooler times, then if you look carefully there appears a little lump upon the finger where the leaf waved its blessings into the world. This is the bud, which contains and offers the promise of life for the following great cycle of time,' he continued.

'What is the promise of life?' asked Rahh, in his best and most enthusiastic student's voice.

Fuff hopped and spun into a flurry of colour and then settled again.

'You ask good questions, Rahh. You are my student and I will teach you,' he said. 'The promise of life is the greatest gift that has ever been given to all creatures that have a beating heart. It goes beyond the limited words of the forest to describe it. You can only know the promise of life when your heart is fully opened and then it is the most wonderful thing that can be experienced by any living thing.'

'As you sit here before me in the magical garden of the healers, even though you are sitting still, everything inside you is moving. It is living with the magic of life,' said Fuff. 'If you look at your chest, Rahh, it rises and falls with the air that goes in and out of your nose and mouth. Do you see it?'

Rahh looked and saw his fur moving up and down.

'Oh yes, I can see my fur moving,' he said.

'Well, it is not so much moving up and down but expanding and contracting. A great part of your body called lungs expands and pulls in the air, which contains the promise of life. The air is called the 'Great Invisibility' and fills your insides with the magic of the healers and the buds. This invisibility fills you with the promise of life. Every tiny second that you are here upon the Mother, you take into yourself the promise of life.'

Rahh suddenly felt that he was being filled up again, not so much with the promise of life but with information that was too big for a small rabbit. Fuff saw the strain in Rahh's thoughts and said to him, 'Rahh, I think you need to eat some breakfast grass.'

The little bunny's eyes lit up with joy. 'How clever you are, Fuff! How did you know that I was ready for my breakfast grass?' he asked.

'Did you forget that I can see your thoughts, Rahh? They float out of you into the great invisibility where I see them,' said Fuff.

'Oh, yes, I had quite forgotten, but now I see what a wonderful thing that is, because you know exactly when I need to eat breakfast or indeed any other meal of the day,' said Rahh.

Fuff laughed and Rahh laughed too.

'Follow me then,' said Fuff. 'I will guide you to a sacred place in the wood where the Great Light falls upon the ground and the grass will be very sweet.'

'Thank you,' said Rahh.

Fuff shot upwards into the invisibility and flitted through the arms of the healers with Rahh chasing after him on the ground. After only a short distance they came upon a lovely glade of fresh, juicy green grass. Looking up Rahh could see the blue like a hole in the woodland roof. In fact, thought Rahh, the woodland is really like a burrow. It can be dark but also if you look up you can see out of the burrow and into the blue. How interesting.

34

The Promise of Life

Rahh was really enjoying the sweet grass this morning. There was something fresh about this day but he was not sure what it was.

'Perhaps it is hearing Fuff's music while I eat?' he thought, but he soon forgot to think about his feelings because the taste of breakfast was so good that it took all his rabbit attention.

By and by, Rahh's tummy was filled with green juice and he noticed that a ray of light fell upon the woodland floor at the edge of the glade.

'I will lie there for a while to allow my breakfast to settle,' he said to himself.

After some time there was a sudden disturbance right in front of his nose as Fuff materialised from within his trembling ball of red and brown fluff. Rahh sat up dreamily and Fuff looked quizzically at him with his head on one side.

'Well, rabbit, are you ready to continue with your work?'

'My work?' questioned Rahh.

'Yes, your work,' said Fuff. 'Your work of learning about the Greatness of Everything.'

'The Greatness of Everything?' queried Rahh, quite alarmed. "Everything' is too much for a rabbit to know. We are small furry creatures with not much intelligence!'

'But you are full of the promise of life, are you not?' said Fuff.

'I am?' asked Rahh.

'Yes, of course,' replied Fuff. 'Let us continue with the wisdom of the woodland. What can you recall from our words before breakfast?'

'Erm, well...' Rahh was still struggling with 'The Greatness of Everything' and how that might be too big for a rabbit, so he couldn't put it out of his mind.

'Are you ready or not?' demanded Fuff, with some of the old impatience in his voice. 'There is much work to do and I am sure that I would not have had this much trouble with the Golden Rabbit I was supposed to teach.'

Rahh felt pain in his fur at being told off but also the pain of hearing Golden Rabbit's name; for a moment he felt that he would never get over losing her. Fuff could see Rahh's thoughts and realised how sensitive and delicate the rabbit really was.

'I am very sorry, Rahh. I ask your forgiveness,' he said.

'There is no need,' Rahh replied. 'I know it is my own pain and I will endure it until I have learned all the lessons it can teach me. Eventually, it will melt away.' He took a deep breath. 'I think I am ready to continue: I am the student again, like I was with Golden Rabbit and you must be here to teach me.'

Fuff suddenly bounced high into the invisibility and words poured out of him that took Rahh quite by surprise.

'I am that which flies above the world,
I am that which sees the truth,
I am that which feels all the love that is everywhere,
And I am that which opens the eyes that wish to see.'

'I am that which only wishes to share the glory that I have seen in our precious world,' Fuff went on. 'I will gladly share my love, my knowledge and my wisdom of experience with any creature who would care to sit and hear.'

Rahh watched the creature carefully. He could see that Fuff was indeed full of something: whether it was berries, buds or wisdom, he was not sure, but he did believe he meant well.

Rahh sat up in his best student position and paid great attention. 'I am ready to sit and hear your wisdom,' he said.

'Thank you, Rahh. Now where were we? Ah yes, let us put

[146]

aside the big picture of the Greatness of Everything and deal with one small step at a time. That will be easy for a small rabbit to understand. Yes, we will approach the Greatness of Everything one small rabbit step at a time. Hmmm. Yes,' said Fuff thoughtfully. 'What can you recall from our words before breakfast?' he asked Rahh once more.

'We were speaking about the buds being the Children of the Forest and containing and offering the Promise of Life. They appear when the leaves leave the ends of the fingers of the healers,' said Rahh.

'Very good,' said Fuff.

'And you said that the Children of the Forest are more than any countist can count,' said Rahh.

'Yes, that is correct Rahh. It is amazing you can remember all this after you have eaten a full breakfast,' joked Fuff, and Rahh chuckled too.

Rahh continued. 'Then you spoke about the wind spirit, who comes to help take the cloak of summer from the healers, and the world turns colder at the end of the great cycle of light. At that time the healers call to sister wind to help them to lay their cloak of wonderful colours onto the earth. Then the fingers of the tall beings are bare but those with eyes can see the promise of life,' said Rahh.

'Rahhhh!' shouted Fuff, as he spun into a fizzy fit and shot vertically into the air. Rahh almost jumped out of his skin in alarm and wondered what he had said wrong to elicit such a profound and excited response from the flapping fizzer.

Fuff descended gracefully and looking into the frightened rabbit's eyes, said 'I am so impressed, Rahh. You are so full of mystery. You are a small rabbit to look at but full of wisdom yourself to know all of these things. You are a magical rabbit and a king of the forest.'

Rahh, still quite alarmed, replied, 'But you told them to me this morning!'

'Ah, yes, I did tell them to you, but you remembered all those wonderful and complex things, Rahh. You remembered a part of the story of the Promise of Life and that means you have the knowledge inside you now,' said Fuff.

'However, true knowledge comes from experience,' he went on. 'You must learn how to see and experience these things, Rahh, and that gives you real and true knowledge, which is also the knowledge of truth. Yes, I am impressed with you, Rahh. Do you recall what the Promise of Life is, Rahh?'

'It is the great invisibility that makes your fur go up and down,' said Rahh.

'Yes, that is correct Rahh. The air that flows into your nose and mouth that makes your fur grow and shrink,' he said, hopping from one foot to the other.

'The Promise of Life is invisible, Rahh. It lives in the great invisibility and some say that it is indeed the great invisibility itself. All beings drink it into themselves every second that their spirit chooses to live in this world.'

'But the Promise of Life is yet to be born each moment that we wait for it, Rahh. Even when we are unaware and not waiting it is preparing itself for us,' said Fuff. He stopped hopping and was very serious, looking deeply into Rahh's eyes as he continued.

'When the Great Light begins once more to fill the blue with its warmth and the light times stretch out like a rabbit's long legs, the buds watch all creatures carefully,' said Fuff. 'They wait and wait and watch and wait,' he went on, looking so deeply into Rahh now that the little rabbit could feel a fire growing in his belly.

'The Children of the Forest are full of excitement to bring forth the promise of life into your fur, Rahh, so that your fur may go up and down and in and out,' said Fuff, with great enthusiasm in his words. 'When we met you had been in the darkness; but upon hearing my music you came out of the dark and noticed that the green blades of sweet grass were once more coming forth from the Mother. Do you recall?'

'Yes, that is so,' said Rahh.

'All beings must rest. Some rest each night and slip into other worlds and some enter the sleeping phase for many cycles of the Great Light. Mother is like that, Rahh; she sleeps for a long time. When she is rested, she then calls to the Great Light to return. As he bathes her with his warmth and light, she calls the droplets that fall from the blue and they pour down upon her. Together, Mother, Father and the droplets wash through all the seeds in the earth and the Promise of Life begins to wake,' said Fuff.

'At the same time, the healers call to mother to bring forth moisture to drink. She brings forth the flowing waters of life from her bosom and they suck it up through their roots, filling themselves with the joy of Mother. The Great Light shines upon the buds and all these things come together to open the Promise of Life,' he went on.

Rahh heard each word so deeply in his heart that he did not notice that already it was past lunchtime and his tummy was calling to be filled again.

'Think about the buds, Rahh. The Children of the Forest. Each one sits and waits for the Mother to feed them the water of life through their parent, the healer. Each time the Great Light passes it hangs longer in the blue and the children grow. They become filled with energy to share their love and beauty. The child eventually cannot hold the pressure any longer and it bursts open, unfolding into the most wonderful expression of love. This expression of love is called a leaf, and as soon as it is born it dances to the hum of the wind spirit for the whole of its life,' said Fuff.

'As each leaf unfolds they join together in the song of love, which forms the great cloak of the healers. The leaves are also the colour of love, which is green. It is the same colour as the light around your heart, Rahh. So when you look into the great healers of the forest they show you that they bring forth love into the world through their wonderfully coloured cloak. Also, you can see the colour of love in every blade of sweet grass that you eat in your morning breakfast.'

'As you see, the mother offers us love in many ways and it is up to each of us to drink it in. The love is offered but it is up to us to take it, receive it and give thanks,' said Fuff.

'Now is the most important part of this mystery, Rahh. As the leaf unfolds, The Promise of Life is finally given for all creatures whose hearts beat with the joy of living.'

Rahh was licking his lips unconsciously in anticipation of receiving the Promise of Life. His heart was hanging on every word that Fuff spoke.

'Now, before we see the promise, Rahh, I think I need to have some more breakfast,' said Fuff.

'Let us rest for a while and I will take myself into the woods and seek the food of the healers to restore my energy. You may rest, or walk or do whatever you wish for a while and contemplate this great story of life,' said Fuff.

Upon that, Fuff burst into a fluttering flurry of colour and disappeared, as if in a puff of smoke.

Rahh just continued to sit, unable to move with the excitement of this revelation. He looked into the tall beings, full of awe and reverence and wishing greatly to see their cloak of green love unfurl from the buds that he could now see clearly at the ends of their fingers.

35

The Great Mystery

Presently, Fuff returned. By this time Rahh had become hungry again and eaten some luncheon grass. He had also popped in and out of here and there and spent some time looking up at these great, tall beings. He could see clearly the buds filled with the promise of life. As he ventured out a little further, learning the way of this new wood, he always returned to the glade so that he did not lose himself, which by some kind of magic still had some sunlight in it.

'Have you eaten?' he asked Fuff.

'Yes, Rahh,' he replied, 'I am now filled with the sweet red berries that I love so much at this time of the day. It has been a wonderful time beneath the Great Light in the blue with you for company.'

He continued, 'I am pleased you want to learn how to see with eyes that see and hear with ears that hear. Would you like to continue, or shall we leave the teaching until another day?'

'Oh let us continue now please! I would love to hear how the Promise of Life is given,' said Rahh.

'Very well. Make yourself comfortable.'

At that moment, Rahh did a very strange thing in the eyes of Fuff. He rolled over onto his back and gazed into the blue.

'What are you doing, Rahh? You have become upside-down with your feet the wrong way up,' he exclaimed.

'Yes, that is correct,' said Rahh. 'I wish to put my ears upon the Mother and look up at the great healers of the woodland whilst I hear your words about the Promise of Life. I feel that I will be more connected with the greatness of everything if I position myself in this way.'

Fuff was again impressed by the inventive wisdom of Rahh. 'That is very interesting, Rahh. I will continue, but do I address myself to your feet or to your ears?'

'You may address me any way that suits you best but it will surely be my ears that hear your words,' said Rahh with a chuckle.

Fuff saw that this was indeed both funny and the truth.

'Ah yes, Rahh, indeed, you would not be hearing these words with any other part of your body! This is the great wisdom of the rabbit speaking,' said Fuff, and they both laughed.

Fuff fluttered and flurried, spun around in a mass of blurred colour and then stood still. Rahh was listening and watching with an upside-down eye.

'LIFE. That is the point we have been coming to all day, Rahh,' said Fuff.

'Life is nothing more than a promise and these wonderful, tall beings that make up the forest are the bearers of that promise.'

Fuff suddenly said, 'Tell me what you see, Rahh.'

This reminded Rahh of when Golden Rabbit had taught him how to see all that long time ago.

'I see everything,' he replied.

'How do you see it?' asked Fuff.

'I see it with my eyes, even though they are upside-down,' said Rahh.

'But what do you see with your heart?' Fuff asked.

'I am not sure if I see anything with my heart,' said Rahh. 'It is inside me and I don't think that it can see out.'

'What can you see with your mind?' asked Fuff.

'I am not sure,' Rahh mused. 'I thought it was in my head but Golden Rabbit told me that it is everywhere; but no matter where it is, I don't think that I can see out of that either.'

'Rahh, you see the Great Light rise into the blue each morning and fall back in the evening. You see it with your eyes but you feel the truth of it with your heart,' said Fuff.

'Behind the cycles of the Great Light and the cycles of all

things, like the cloak of the healers being born and later falling to earth, is a Great Mystery. The centre of the Great Mystery is in your heart, but your heart is also at the centre of the Great Mystery,' said Fuff.

Rahh rolled over and sat up the right way. He could feel the truth of this but didn't understand it properly and it made him dizzy. He repeated Fuff's words.

'The centre of the Great Mystery is in my heart, but my heart is also at the centre of the Great Mystery. Is that right?' he asked.

'Yes, that is correct Rahh,' said Fuff.

'This makes me dizzy Fuff. How can one thing be in another, but the other is inside the first thing. That would mean that both of them are in each other but also outside of each other at the same time. Ohhh, this causes me much rabbit confusion. Can you please explain that to me,' asked Rahh.

'Yes, of course Rahh. When your heart awakens it can see, just like your eyes. I can see with my heart into your heart. That is how I see your thoughts and your pain,' said Fuff.

'When your heart is fully open it exists in more than one place at once. You cannot really understand this until it happens, and then you understand it by knowing the truth of it. It is the process of becoming,' said Fuff.

'There is that 'becoming' word again,' thought Rahh. 'Perhaps I will understand it one day.'

Fuff continued, 'Once you become, then you will see all things in the Great Mystery. You will see beyond everything that your eyes see. You will see things that you will not believe, but still you will know them to be true. The Great Mystery lies behind all things. It is like the Great Light in the blue. It lights up everything with life.'

'Even the Great Light?' asked Rahh.

'Yes, even the Great Light itself,' nodded Fuff.

'It must be very bright to be able to light up the Great Light,' said Rahh.

'Indeed, you cannot look upon it with your eyes, but your heart can see it,' said Fuff. 'But for now all that you have is not life, Rahh, but the promise of life and nothing more.'

Rahh continued to gaze into Fuff's tiny brown eyes and waited for him to speak again.

'When all of the buds which hold the promise of life open, they create a wonderful, new green cloak throughout the Forest of Life. As each cycle of light rises through the dawn, the Great Light in the blue shines upon the green cloak of love. Each leaf in the cloak then sends forth waves of the sweet invisibility.'

At this, Rahh really did not know what to think, but asked a very clever question.

'Can I see this invisibility with my heart?'

'That is a great question,' said Fuff. 'But the answer is not important at the moment. What is important is that when the wind spirit goes into your nose and mouth and your lungs fill with the morning scent of the woodland, this is the moment that the promise of life enters you, Rahh.'

'The green cloak sends out waves of love, which some creatures call air. If you choose to take this air into your lungs, then you have received the gift of the promise of life. But Rahh, this is not life itself. It is only the promise of life.'

Fuff fluttered as if rearranging his disorganised feathers; Rahh wondered how this creature could fly anyway, with such a dishevelled coat.

'As you take in the promise of life when it is offered, certainly your body will move and your fur go up and down, Rahh. But this is not life. It is only animation.'

'Animation?' queried Rahh.

'Yes. Animation just means that you move around the earth carrying your sleeping spirit with you, like some old package of fallen leaves,' said Fuff.

'Your life comes, the days pass and eventually you enter the long rabbit sleep having only eaten the green grass from one garden, having only dwelt within one burrow and only felt the Great Light on your fur and not in your heart.'

'But if you are awake when you take in the promise of life, then it will go deep within you and find your heart. Then you are on your path to create a great life of wakefulness,' said Fuff.

'The promise of life feeds your heart and it becomes stronger. As your heart becomes stronger, the promise of life searches through your body for any part that wishes to hear the words of the Great Mystery; and the Great Mystery promises you a life beyond life and a never ending life as you become,' said Fuff.

'What will I become?' asked Rahh.

'You will become a part of the Great Mystery itself and the Great Mystery will become you. You and the Great Mystery will become one. That is the becoming.'

'Then you will create with every thought and word that you think and speak, and you will become one of the greatest rabbits ever to walk amongst the tall healers of the great forest, Rahh.'

'You will be filled with the promise of life and the Great Mystery all at the same time, and you will shine like the Great Light in the blue. All the beings of the woodlands and fields will know you by your sign – the light within you. They will know that your heart has opened and is pure, and that the Great Mystery filled it with endless promises,' said Fuff.

'At that point you will become a messenger, bringing the Great Mystery into your world for all those who wish to taste its promises. But remember, promises are not life, they are promises. They are the potential to make life great and if you set your focus to be a bringer of the Great Mystery, so you will become it. That is the promise of life,' Fuff explained.

Rahh sat silent and respectful of this small red and brown creature who seemed suddenly to have so much wisdom, knowledge and power that it had completely taken over the whole forest. It was as if all things were listening to the little ball of feathers. There was a total silence but more than that, there was peace throughout the woodland that could not be described in any thoughts or words that Rahh knew. But he could feel the truth of it.

'Perhaps this was the Great Mystery listening and being listened to at the same time,' he thought.

36

The Lights of Heaven

As Rahh sat in the peace and stillness, Fuff held his gaze. No words could be spoken for to speak would be to shatter the stillness and so Rahh sat and Fuff stood in front of him until the Great Light streamed towards mother. Rahh could not move and Fuff did not want to move. They merely gazed into each other's eyes.

Eventually, the shadows in the wood grew longer and the light in the glade had faded, whilst the green of the new grass had become dull with the lack of colour. The Great Light was returning quickly towards his wife, our Mother Earth.

Fuff shook and flurried his feathers and without a word took off in a blur into the arms of the healers above. Rahh looked around and thought that this must be the signal that it was complete, although he wasn't really sure what was complete?

Rahh became aware that Fuff was moving deeper into the woodland and wondered what to do. Should he follow or should he stay where he was? He thought for a moment and decided that he wanted to go back under the bush and prepare his bed for the dark time that was approaching. It was getting cooler and he had much to think about.

Rahh sniffed around the ground and took a few blades of grass for his comfort should he become hungry in the night. He folded his ears back and ducked beneath the branches of the bush, stepping into the small bed that he had made for himself at the last dark time. It was already cosy as it fitted his shape. He placed the blades of grass so that he could find them if he woke up in the dark and was hungry, then he settled.

Rahh decided to lie upon his back and gaze upwards through the branches of the bush to do some blue-sky thinking, even though the blue was now almost black. There was much to ponder. Today Fuff had explained some of the things that Golden Rabbit had spoken about but always saying that he would find out soon enough. Now Fuff had spoken of what becoming was and told him what his sign was, and of course, the most amazing words that opened his eyes and ears to the promise of life and how it all worked. It was indeed a great mystery and he didn't really understand it yet. He had only heard it spoken of but yet he could feel something different inside himself. As if Fuff's words were moving about inside him.

Rahh closed his eyes and gave a thought to where Fuff had gone; but he thought to himself that perhaps Fuff needed to take in some of the invisibility after the great work of explaining all these things.

Rahh also felt quite pleased with himself as he had not collapsed under the great weight of words, but had been able to take them all in. Perhaps he was getting stronger, he thought, or perhaps he was growing in some way.

The wind spirit was gentle, cooing through the arms of the healers and Rahh thought about all the buds preparing themselves to open into the green loving cloaks that would bring the gift of the promise of life that would pour with invisibility from the green leaves. This thing called air. He felt his heart suddenly fill with joy and he opened his eyes to see that there were hundreds of tiny specks of light in the bush. It was a magical sight like he had never seen before.

As these lights sprinkled him with their mystery he heard the sound of Fuff's music far off in the distance, singing the praises of the Great Light in the blue and giving thanks for every beam of light that falls upon the earth and all who live and dwell here. That reminded Rahh to also give thanks for the day and all it had given to him.

The gathering dark time was not frightening at all to Rahh but felt like a warm cloak of straw holding him safe. The tiny lights were now much brighter and covered the whole of the darkness. He realised now that they were not in the bush at all but this must be Heaven that he had heard about as they were very high up where the blue should be. The beauty was overwhelming and he felt his heart move and joyful tears tumbled from his eyes.

'Perhaps I am feeling the great mystery,' he thought. The vision was beautiful but also caused him pain as the tears came. He remembered Golden Rabbit's words the first time he had felt this kind of pain.

'Is it painful, Rahh?' asked Golden Rabbit. 'Does it hurt inside?'

'Yes,' said Rahh. 'Why do I hurt so much? What is happening to me?'

Golden Rabbit said, 'You are Becoming.'

Rahh thought that the specks of light must be like the buds, far too many to count. As he was thinking about how to count he was slowly taken into the dreamtime, with the lights of heaven bathing his life and the words of Golden Rabbit swimming through his heart.

'You are Becoming.'

37

The Rumbling Earth

Rahh awoke to feel the earth rumbling beneath him. It was still the dark time outside and there was no music from Fuff yet. He lay still, feeling the movement in the earth; it was shaking him and he was trembling inside at the same time.

He was still on his back in the position in which he had fallen asleep, gazing at the lights of heaven but now he rolled over onto his tummy. He placed his paws and one ear on the ground, listening to and feeling the shaking earth. Inside him the trembling was as if his tummy was rumbling violently with hunger but it was quite a different feeling.

With his ear to the ground Rahh became aware of footsteps padding towards where he lay under the bush. He heard a nose sniffing. He lay very still, listening.

'Is this creature causing the earth to rumble and shake beneath me?' he thought. The sniffing came closer and stopped just outside. Then a nose appeared under the bush where Rahh's bed was. He kept perfectly still.

A tongue came out and licked the nose and then the nose pushed deeper under the bush towards Rahh. Suddenly, Rahh's body leapt in the air and flew out of the bush in a great roar.

A huge red creature jumped backwards through the air before coming to land on its belly with its legs pointing in all directions.

Rahh roared a command at the beast: 'Get back, you foolish creature! Would you disturb the fires of all the dragons in the forest?'

He was quite startled by his inner lion which seemed to be much more active now than ever before. His whole body shook, which seemed to make the roar louder and more powerful. His whiskers were shaking so much that he thought they might fall out.

The great red creature was completely startled. He tried to stand up but his legs were so wobbly that he couldn't, so he just lay there looking at Rahh.

Rahh took a step forward and another huge roar came out of him and the huge red creature put his paws over his eyes. 'Please do not bring the dragon fire upon me,' it moaned.

'Who are you?' roared Rahh.

'I...I...I am Red Fox and this is my trail. I am sorry to disturb you.'

Rahh knew about the red creatures and that if you were not careful they would eat a rabbit up so he knew he had to be bold.

'Today, Red Fox, it is your lucky day, for I will not bring the dragon fire upon you if you leave this wood and never return. This is where I live and there is not enough room for the dragon fire and you,' he roared.

'I am terribly sorry to have disturbed you. I will go back the way I came and never come this way again. That is my promise,' said Red Fox.

'Very well then, but be aware that the dragon fire lives in this wood; you had better warn any other creatures that are intent on mischief not to come this way,' Rahh threatened.

Red Fox's legs sprang upwards he found his feet and ran, barking loudly into the darkness.

Rahh was in such a panic that he shot back under the bush shaking with something. He didn't know what it was but he knew that it wasn't the rabbit fear, which surprised him. He suddenly felt vulnerable and alone. He pulled the leaves up around him and lay shivering and shaking upon the earth and wondered when the Great Light would be coming.

Then he noticed that Fuff was fast asleep in the bush above him and hadn't heard or seen anything. 'How could that be?' thought Rahh, but decided that he wouldn't wake him up now. Surely the Great Light will be coming soon.

38

Red Fox

Presently, Rahh heard Fuff's music in the distance. He realised that he must have eventually gone back to sleep after his encounter with Red Fox. In fact, he wondered if had he met him in the dream time and was really not sure if the whole event had taken place at all.

Rahh was not in a hurry to rise from his bed and continued to lay there in the cosy burrow. He was most definitely a little dazed: so much had happened during this last cycle of the light and dark time. He was thinking and wondering about all the things that Fuff had said yesterday and also about Red Fox, the roaring lion and the dragon fire. He was so deeply pondering all these big things that he didn't realise Fuff was actually looking down at him from on top of the bush.

'Oh – good morning Fuff,' he said.

'Good morning, Rahh. What is this, still in your bed and it is almost past breakfast time? Are you not hungry this morning?'

'I had not even heard my tummy calling. It is as if I am full up,' said Rahh.

'Did you sneak out in the night and eat dark grass then?' asked Fuff.

'No, I didn't eat anything, but I did go outside,' said Rahh, still looking over his shoulder and up through the bush.

'You went outside in the dark time?' said Fuff, with some alarm in his voice. 'Do you not know there are creatures roaming in the dark time who will eat a rabbit if they get the chance?'

'Yes, I do know it,' said Rahh. 'I think I met one last night.'

'You think you met one? Who did you meet?'

'I met Red Fox,' said Rahh calmly.

'Red Fox!' Fuff's alarm was reaching a crescendo that made him hop three times his own height, spin round and land again. 'You met Red Fox and are still here to tell the tale? Rahh, this must have been a dream, as Red Fox would have eaten you up.'

'I am not sure if I was dreaming or not ... but wait a minute: if it was true, the grass will be flattened where he lay down in front of me,' said Rahh.

'Where he *lay down in front of you*?!' repeated Fuff in disbelief.

'Yes, I will come out and have a look,' said Rahh.

Rahh nipped from his bed under the bush popping out into the open.

'Look there Fuff, the grass is flattened,' said Rahh.

Fuff flew down to the ground to inspect the area. 'Rahh, you are right. I can smell Red Fox but do you know who he is?'

'No, I just knew that he would eat me if I was not careful,' replied Rahh.

'Red Fox is king of the woodland at night. Not only that, he is the biggest, strongest fox in all the fox kingdom. He is the King of the Foxes, Rahh. How is it that you were not eaten?'

Rahh proceeded to tell Fuff about how the earth was shaking and he had woken up and was listening to it and feeling it, when he heard the footsteps approaching, and of course, the sniffing nose.

He then told Fuff how the lion had come roaring out of him, but instead of just his whiskers shaking, his whole body was shaking and that his whole body had flown out from under the bush right under the nose of Red Fox. Then how Red Fox had jumped so far up in the air and backwards that his legs all gave way when he landed. Rahh added that it was quite funny to see. And then of course, how Red Fox couldn't stand up because his legs were shaking so much.

'You made Red Fox's legs shake, Rahh?' asked Fuff, with eyes wide open.

'Well, they were shaking but I have no idea if I made that happen,' said Rahh. 'My ears stood up in the air and my body took a leap towards him and the roaring came out of me again, even louder. Then there was a smell of burning and Red Fox covered his eyes with his paws and said, 'Please do not bring the dragon fire upon me."

'Ahh, now I understand,' said Fuff, excitedly. 'I understand why you were not eaten by Red Fox.'

'Tell me, please!' asked Rahh.

'I will explain,' said Fuff, 'but not before we have eaten a fine breakfast together, Rahh. You can tell me the rest of your story on the way. You great little rabbit!' he chuckled.

Suddenly, Fuff leapt into the air and did one of those spinning things where he became a blur of red and brown. He flapped, whistled and hooted all at the same time and seemed to be extremely excited. Then he suddenly sung out to the woodland, 'Look at my friend the Great Rabbit who chased away the King of the Foxes! Let all the forest know that the Red Fox beater lives in this wood. All should be aware and all should be wary,' he howled, with great joy and enthusiasm in his voice.

'Come, Rahh, the Great Light has already been in the blue for a long time and is almost at its zenith. By the time we have eaten breakfast it will be time to eat supper,' said Fuff.

Fuff turned, hopped and took to the air and Rahh chased after him.

39

The Red Pool

Fuff led Rahh to the edge of the wood where the Great Light in the blue was already high and warming the grass. Fuff hopped about in the bushes on the edge of the wood while Rahh nibbled fresh green shoots just inside this new field that he had not seen before. He noted that it was facing east, the way they had to go in order to begin a new journey. As he nibbled the grass the Great Light warmed his face and he could also see many jewels in the morning dew, which lifted his spirits even more – if that were possible.

When thirst and hunger had been quenched, Fuff flew down and landed in front of Rahh. 'Follow me,' he said.

Fuff hopped and flurried, flipped and flitted across the field. Rahh followed and presently they came to a sheet of water lying in a dip in the field. Rahh had never seen water looking so lovely. It was all blue like the blue above.

Fuff stood in front of Rahh and suddenly spun into one of his blurred, speedy images, all red and brown with feathers sticking out here and there. He stopped, hopped twice and looked into Rahh's eyes.

'Today, Rahh, you are the Greatest Rabbit who ever lived.'

Fuff lifted his wings up high and wide in a gesture to indicate how big and great Rahh had become.

Rahh was bewildered as he had no idea what Fuff was talking about. 'What do you mean?' he asked.

'I mean that you, a singular rabbit of little worldly knowledge or experience frightened away the most fearsome and terrible fox that the woodland has ever known. All creatures will bow down to you when they hear this news and already I have sung it through the arms of the great Healers so all creatures will indeed know very soon.'

Rahh was not sure about this. 'What if Red Fox comes back to eat me once he has recovered his courage?' he asked.

'There is no doubt, he will not return,' said Fuff.

'How are you so sure?' asked Rahh.

'This is how I know,' said Fuff. 'You spoke to me about the earth rumbling beneath you and it woke you up. Then you listened to it with an ear on the ground, which made you shake and tremble. Is that right, Rahh?'

'Oh yes indeed, yes, the shaking and trembling was quite terrible. I was very worried until I heard the footsteps padding softly towards me,' said Rahh.

'It was the truth in your words that I heard and then Red Fox's answer, which confirmed to me what was happening – you said to him, 'Would you disturb the fires of all the dragons in the forest?' And he replied, 'Please do not bring the Dragon Fire upon me.''

'Yes, but what does it mean?' asked Rahh. He could remember Zzard speaking about the Dragon Fire that time when he thought Zzard would eat Golden Rabbit.

'You see my bright red feathers, Rahh?' said Fuff, pushing his chest out.

'Yes, I see them, they are a wonderful colour.'

'This is the sign of the Dragon Fire. I have been blessed with it,' said Fuff proudly.

'What is the Dragon Fire?' Rahh questioned.

'You are my student and I will tell you,' said Fuff.

Rahh thought that he was going to follow this statement with something about going for food again, or wait until tomorrow, as the Great Light was already falling but that was not the case.

'Look into the waters of the pool, Rahh, and tell me what you see,' said Fuff.

'Oh, I know this game now,' thought Rahh, 'I am supposed to see something that I can't normally see so I will look very hard and show Fuff how clever I am.'

So Rahh looked into the still, glassy waters of the pool but as much as he looked he could only see water, which was as blue as the blue above.

'I can only see the water, which is as blue as the blue above,' he said.

'That is very good, Rahh. Do you know why the water is so blue?'

'I don't think I do but it is most perfectly the same blue as the blue above,' the little rabbit replied.

'That is because it *is* the same blue!' laughed the creature, giving a little hop and a jig. 'The waters are reflecting the blue from above and bringing it down to us below. As it is above, so shall it be below, if you know how to see it. What you see is something that not many in this world can see,' Fuff said.

Rahh looked at the creature in a quizzical way and said, 'But I am seeing what all creatures who stand here would see.'

'No, that is not the case,' said Fuff. 'What you are seeing is something deeper. You are seeing the truth of the Great Mystery.'

Rahh felt the rabbit confusion coming on. One minute he was the greatest living rabbit in history, and now he was quickly reverting to a confused rabbit who wanted to go to his burrow, except that he didn't have one yet. Well, not a proper one.

'The Great Mystery?' he said.

'Yes. When I was sent to your burrow, I was told by the spirit of the Great Mystery to bring the Golden Rabbit to this pool of reflections and to give the creature a key that opens one of the doors of the Great Mystery,' said Fuff.

'But Golden Rabbit was not there, she had gone,' said Rahh.

'That is correct,' said Fuff. 'But you are also this amazing and wonderful rabbit, even though you are not golden…And because of what happened last night with Red Fox I feel that I must also show you this key, so that you will understand what happened when you put the fear into him.'

'Soon I will show you the truth of the reflection, but let us rest a while first. It is already late in the cycle of light and soon the Great Light will bow his head towards his wife and settle with her for the dark time. Let us sit and watch the reflections of truth in the still waters of this ocean of wisdom,' said Fuff, pointing into the pool with his beak.

Rahh felt that perhaps he should not ask any more questions, but just do as he was bid and look towards the pool. He made himself comfortable and looked down his nose at his own whiskers to amuse himself as they sat and sat for quite a while.

Presently Fuff spoke.

'The time is almost with us, Rahh. We must sit opposite the Great Light as he tumbles towards the Earth, so that we see both him and his reflection in the ocean of wisdom, this pool.'

Rahh and Fuff positioned themselves opposite the Great Light and watched patiently but without looking directly into the light because it was too bright. The Great Light began to turn from white to yellow and then to orange.

'Watch carefully now, Rahh, whilst I sit opposite you on the other side of the pool.' Fuff took up his position facing Rahh across the pool and Rahh watched Fuff as the pool turned from orange to deep red. The radiance of the Great Light bounced off the pool in all directions, even lighting up the red feathers on Fuff's breast.

His feathers began to grow brighter as if turning to fire and the red fire transformed into a red and golden light. Fuff seemed to be growing bigger and Rahh instinctively took a few steps backwards, shielding his eyes a little from the light.

There was a sudden enormous crack, like when the blue turns

[168]

black and is split by light and the roaring noise. The crack was so sharp, Rahh jumped back in shock, closing his eyes for a second.

The earth began to rumble and shake and the red and gold light flickered and flashed around Fuff as the pool turned from calm to angry. Too much was changing too quickly for a small rabbit and Rahh didn't know whether to run or dig a quick burrow but certainly he didn't want to be here any longer. He looked up again to see Fuff suddenly consumed with fire and disappearing in a flashing image of himself.

Another huge crack split the air and Rahh winced and cowered, trembling at the sound of it. As he opened his eyes again, there were huge wings where Fuff had been standing. There was a great roar like the earth was coming to an end and Rahh tried to become invisible with his paws over his eyes and his ears laid back.

The earth shook ten times greater than before and as Rahh peeped once more the great wings rose upwards and a huge red dragon appeared in front of him across the pool. It towered into the blazing red heavens, a hundred times taller than he was. It looked down, piercing him with blazing golden eyes.

Rahh's body leapt into the air by itself and as he landed ran round in a circle quite terrified, not knowing which way to go. He had never felt the rabbit fear this strongly but somehow it was quite nice to know it was still with him at this moment. Just as he was about to run for the wood the air cracked again as the wings began to beat.

'Poor Fuff never had a chance,' thought Rahh. The heat from this monster was unbearable. Each time the huge wings beat downwards the air cracked again. The dragon's massive head was rolling and roaring in all directions, its long neck twisting like a snake in torment. It seemed as if the beast writhed and slithered into life as it drove itself upwards into the blue with the loudest roar he had ever heard. The blue of course, was now completely red from the Great Light sinking into oblivion.

A host of black-winged creatures flew from the woodland crying in fear and the ground felt like it would open up and swallow Rahh whole.

Rahh stayed low in the grass not knowing what to do, so he just lay there hardly daring to peep. After climbing, the dragon roared downwards out of the red and swooped low across the pool directly towards Rahh. At the last second it pulled its head up just skimming Rahh's ears. The heat from its breath was incredible and the grass around him steamed as the dragon soared upwards over the top of the woodland and out of sight.

Rahh opened his eyes and wondered whether to run for the woodland or not. Part of his body wanted to run but nothing seemed to be working in his legs.

All went quiet but before he had time to pull his legs under him to run, he saw fire pouring through the wood coming straight towards him. The healers were lit up almost as bright as the Great Light, but red, and now Rahh could actually see a fire ball blazing through the woodland.

The fire ball burst out of the woodland with the dragon behind it. Rahh could see the fire coming out of its mouth and its wings seemed to be made of fire too. This whole blazing, roaring, terrifying sight and sound was coming directly at him again but this time at an impossible speed.

It skimmed over his ears and he smelt the fire and felt the heat once more. It rose again into the air, turned in a dramatic circle and then landed on the opposite side of the pool to Rahh.

Rahh's whiskers were steaming and one eye was still covered by a paw as he gingerly peeped out of the other one. The beast's golden eyes pierced Rahh to the point where he felt like he was cooking on the inside.

It lowered its head, its eyes still holding Rahh's singular gaze. It reached its long neck forward and pierced the now calm pool with its tongue. The water hissed and boiled and a cloud of steam rose into the air as the dragon pulled his head back again.

Rahh was held tightly in its gaze. He couldn't look away and both his eyes were now wide open. He could see the reflection of the dragon in the pool, which was as real as the one opposite him on the other bank.

'What do you see, Rahhhhhh?' said the dragon in a fiery roar that made Rahh tremble and shake like the night before.

Rahh's terror came back. 'It knows my name. It has come for me,' he thought.

'Do not be afraid, Rahh, but tell me what you see,' said the dragon again.

'I...I...I am not sure. I think I see a dragon, but I am confused and terrified, so I am not sure,' Rahh squeaked.

The dragon continued to pierce him with his golden gaze, fire licking upwards round its mouth. Rahh was certainly wanting to run again when the dragon raised its head a little and asked the same question.

'Tell me what you see, Rahhhhhh!!'

'I...I...I do not know. If it is not a dragon, I do not know, please tell me what I see,' said Rahh, unable really to answer any kind of question at this time.

'What you see, Rahh,' the Dragon hesitated, waiting for Rahh's full attention.

'What you see, Rahh...is your Mother,' it said.

Rahh closed his eyes in fear again. 'How can this vision of terrifying fire be my mother?' he thought, and said without looking, 'How are you my mother?'

'You are my student and I will tell you,' said the dragon, roaring again with such ferocity that the earth shook and trembled at its voice.

'Even my mother the earth shakes in fear of you,' shouted Rahh above the rumbling sound. His head disappeared deeply into the grass, his eyes remained closed and his ears back to protect them from the deafening sounds and heat. All then went quiet and a stillness and strange silence was all around him. He even felt a gentle peace. He lay for a while beneath his paws, then finally dared to peep out.

The grass was smouldering and smoking and across the pool was a sight he never expected to see. It was Fuff.

Rahh sat up, shaking. 'Where have you been!' he shouted across the pool. 'There was a great and fearsome dragon here. You abandoned me, you ball of brown and red moss!'

Fuff said nothing for a few moments waiting for Rahh's fear and anger to leave him. Then he said, 'I think we better head to the wood, the dark time is upon us, Rahh.'

Rahh had not really noticed that the Great Light had now slipped out of sight, such was the drama that had unfolded in his little furry world these past few moments. At the thought of returning to the wood he was indeed thankful and really couldn't encourage Fuff to move any faster than it was possible to go. 'But what about the dragon that was here?' he asked.

'The dragon is resting now, Rahh,' said Fuff.

'How do you know? Did you see it, Fuff?'

'Yes, I saw it. Now let us hurry across the field so we can get you into your safe bed.'

40

Mother

Rahh was very happy to be underneath the bush and in his cosy little bowl in the ground. He pulled a few leaves close to him and noticed that the blades of grass from the night before were still there. 'I might eat those in a moment,' he thought.

Fuff fluttered into the branches just above Rahh and the two creatures looked at each other.

'You are safe Rahh,' said Fuff.

'But I am worried that Red Fox might come back for me during the night and what about this dragon?' Rahh asked.

'I am the dragon,' said Fuff.

'You! You are not the dragon. You disappeared as soon as the dragon roared out of the fiery red pool,' said Rahh with some alarm in his voice. 'You abandoned me.'

'Be still, Rahh. Take the invisibility into your fur deeply, then let it out slowly and feel the peace around you,' replied Fuff.

Rahh breathed in held it then let it out and was still. It was true, he could feel the peace.

'Is that better, Rahh? Can you feel the peace now?'

'Yes, I can feel it,' he answered.

'The peace is given by Mother to all those who would welcome it into their lives,' said Fuff. 'When you choose to worry then you will feel anxious – but it is a choice. The same with fear. Things may be frightening at times but it is a choice to feel that energy or to feel peace,' said Fuff.

'Thank you, I am in peace now,' said Rahh and leaned forward to eat a blade of green grass.

'I will tell you the truth, Rahh. It will take you some time to prove to yourself that this is the truth, but I am sure you will see it soon. When we stood by the ocean of wisdom what did you see?' asked Fuff.

'I saw so many things before the waters turned angry and rose up. But then I was also entering into the rabbit terror as all the world was turning red,' Rahh answered.

'I will help you, Rahh. It has been a difficult day for you and so now you must rest in the peace and stillness of the dark time in our beautiful wood. I will tell you how things unfolded so that you don't have to work hard to think. It is late and you have had many surprises today.'

'Thank you,' said the little rabbit.

'You saw the Great Light turn red and come down into the pool. That was the fire of life, the Father coming from the heavens to kiss his bride through the window of the great ocean of wisdom, which is nothing more than a pool to other creatures. A place to bathe and drink but those with love in their heart can learn to see beyond the reflections of the surface and into the truth,' said Fuff.

'What you saw, Rahh, was the Great Mystery coming together. When Father and Mother touch there can be a great explosion of energy in those who have trained to hold it,' said Fuff.

'Right in the heart of your Mother is a great pool of liquid fire, just like the pool in the field. It is the fire of life and when she wishes to speak the fire rumbles and the earth shakes.'

'In the last dark time your mother came to help you when Red Fox was coming to your bed. She began to shake you and woke you up with her shaking and trembling to protect you. Once you were awake she put the power of the Dragon Fire into you and you roared fire like a dragon. Even though you did not see it the Dragon Fire came out of your mouth and Red Fox was terrified. He will never, never come this way again and you can be sure he told everyone about the Dragon Rabbit living in the wood,' said Fuff.

[174]

'Yes, he put his paws over his eyes. But why did I not see the Dragon Fire myself?' asked Rahh.

Fuff replied, 'You can only see it with a heart that has become illuminated, Rahh. It is the pure energy of Mother and as you continue to Become, so you will then be able to see how it manifests through you and comes into this world.'

'But what about the dragon in the field; the one that flew up into the air and breathed fire?' asked Rahh, with eyes wide open.

'Look into my eyes, Rahh, and tell me what you see when I speak to you,' said Fuff.

Rahh sat up a little and paid great attention like a good student and Fuff continued.

'When the red light of Father kisses the red fire of Mother, through the window of the ocean of wisdom, those with an open heart will see the gold beyond all other colours. Gold is the sign at the heart of the Great Mystery. The centre of all that is. The greatest part of the greatness of everything,' said Fuff.

Rahh felt how big this was and he could feel the power of it as Fuff spoke.

'I am a keeper of Mother's Dragon Fire. This is the sign upon my breast. When I have dragon work to do, then I call to Mother and Father. They come together in my breast and the burst of energy of his light and her fire transforms me into the dragon. When I speak about the dragon you can see the fire deep within my eyes. Look carefully Rahh, until you see the truth inside my eyes.'

'Yes, I can see the flames burning,' said Rahh.

'The dragon is not a fearful creature; it is full of the love of Mother, but that love is so hot and fiery that it can frighten many creatures until they know it is love. Even the keepers of the Dragon Fire can be afraid of it sometimes as it is so powerful within them. So we have to be very careful and learn how to use it wisely.'

'Last night was a great night for you, Rahh. You are becoming a great rabbit for during the dark time the mother chose you. She blessed you with the gift of the Dragon Fire to save you from Red Fox. The Dragon Fire is now within your heart and it will show itself when you need the help of your Mother,' said Fuff.

'The fire will burn brightly in you and the father will see that you have been chosen by the Mother and he will help you too.'

'How will he help me?' asked Rahh.

'That is not for me to say or to know,' Fuff replied. 'Once you have been chosen and blessed only the mother and father know which path you will walk through the forest of life. But one thing is for certain, Rahh – you will never be alone. They will always walk by your side. They will come together in your heart and bring new life into you. You will never grow old in the spirit as you will always be renewed within.' said Fuff.

'Now, Rahh, look deeply into my eyes and tell me what you see.'

Rahh looked deeper and then he could see the truth of what Fuff had said.

'I can see the truth,' he replied.

'And how does it look, Rahh?' asked Fuff.

'It is the pure gold at the heart of the Great Mystery and it is beautiful. It is the same gold that I saw in the dragon's eyes,' said Rahh.

'Very good, Rahh. Now that you have seen the sign within me, you will be able to see it in any other creature that has been opened into the Great Mystery. You will always be able to see the gold at the centre of the Greatness of Everything,' said Fuff.

'Now, I think we should prepare to sleep. Already the dark time is very black but we can see the lights in the heavens. I would like to sleep next to you tonight Rahh if you would allow it?'

'Of course, that is fine but please tell me why,' said Rahh.

'I would like to feel the Dragon Fire growing within you, warming you and indeed, warming me against these still cold nights,' said Fuff.

'Let it be so. Please, come close to my fur and rest with me,' said Rahh.

And so the creatures settled in a warm aura of awakening Dragon Fire to sleep a deep, deep, healing and awakening sleep.

41

Looking for a Place to Burrow

The Great Light soon rose and Fuff was singing upwards into the blue when Rahh awoke. He stretched, rolled onto his back to scratch and then was almost ready to come out into the world. He lay for a moment, looking up through the branches. He was so pleased that Golden Rabbit had taught him that rabbits can go upside-down. 'It is so interesting to see everything in a different way,' he thought.

But his tummy was calling so he rolled over again and peeped out from under the bush and into the woodland beyond.

'What is this?' he said out loud, as outside his little bushy bedroom were nuts, berries and beautifully cut strands of sweet morning grass. He hopped out and as far as he could see there was food laid out all the way to the sunny glade. He trod carefully through the food, which included exotic leaves that he had never seen before and eventually came to the glade.

He wondered who all the food belonged to and the sight of it made his tummy growl like the lion in his heart. He settled to nibble some sweet morning grass in the glade and presently Fuff appeared.

'Well, Rahh, what do you think of all the glorious bounty of the forest of life?'

'I don't know what to think of it at all. How has it come here? Perhaps someone will come back for it later,' he replied.

'Have you not touched it?' said Fuff, with eyes wide open in surprise. 'But it is yours, Rahh. It is your food.'

'Mine?' exclaimed Rahh. 'Where did it come from?'

'These are all small gifts from the creatures of the woodland for sending away Red Fox. These are gifts of gratitude and thankfulness. I told you that word of your great deed would soon spread,' said Fuff.

'But there is enough here to feed ten rabbits for many cycles of the Great Light!'

'Indeed,' said Fuff. 'You have been welcomed and accepted and I think it is time that you made a home here, Rahh. It is time for you to dig a burrow.'

'But I am a bush rabbit now,' said Rahh. 'I love it under our bush and seeing the lights of Heaven in the dark time with you sitting just above me.'

'Yes, but I think it is important that you dig a burrow, Rahh, and then you can have a larder to place all this food within. The food will keep well underground and you can feed yourself when you have the desire or hunger during the dark time,' said Fuff.

'Ah, yes, that is a good idea to keep the food well,' said Rahh. 'But where will I dig a burrow? In fact, I have never dug a burrow before. I used to live in my parents' burrow and then I lived in a burrow that Golden Rabbit prepared for me, then I lived in Golden Rabbit's burrow where you found me. And now I live under a bush with no fear of Red Fox or other animals of the dark time. Indeed, I have lived in many places already in my short life!'

'Well, I think it is time that you took the great step of creating your own home and then you can decide if you want to sleep in it or not. You must realise Rahh, that you cannot be a proper rabbit until you have dug a burrow,' said Fuff.

'I think you may be right,' said Rahh, feeling a little excitement at the prospect of learning how to make a home for himself.

'I also think it is time that we moved on from this place, Rahh. The forest is huge and we only live in a small part of it called the wood but the forest is everywhere. It is time for us to move on and find a new place for a while,' said Fuff. 'After breakfast, let us gather your gifts and place them in your bed beneath the bush. Nobody will go there because they know that is where the Dragon Rabbit lives. Then we will move forward through the woodland and find a place where you would like to make your burrow,' said Fuff.

'Yes, that sounds like a good plan. I am sure it is time to move on now. Our work seems to be done in this part of the wood,' said Rahh.

Rahh continued to nibble some fine breakfast grass and Fuff bounced hither and thither through the arms of the healers, eating various things that pleased his appetite. After breaking the fast of the dark time they moved Rahh's gifts of food into his bed and set off through the wood. Fuff led the way, flitting and fluffing high and low whilst singing a pleasant morning tune. Rahh followed with his feet firmly on the earth. Sometimes he could see Fuff and at other times Fuff was too far ahead but the sound of his music was always in reach.

As the day drew on and the Great Light began to come down towards Mother, Fuff waited for Rahh.

'This feels like a good place to dwell for a while,' he said.

'Yes, I can feel it is different from where we lived before,' said Rahh.

'Would you like to look around for a fine place to dig your first burrow?' asked Fuff.

'Yes,' replied Rahh, 'I have been thinking about such a place whilst I have been following you through the wood. I notice that the healers are much taller and older now we are deeper into the wood. I think that I would like to ask permission of one of these great beings to live within its roots.'

'That's a good idea Rahh, but why did you choose such a place?' asked Fuff.

'Firstly, there is great strength in these beings and with strength comes love. Also, I would like to be close to the healers. You told me that the animals come to the healers for help and so I would like to burrow in that love and healing energy when I sleep, then it will help to restore me,' the little rabbit replied.

[180]

'Yes, that would be the case, Rahh. Whenever you are near the healers if you take time to sit with them they will always help you; they are so intelligent and, as you say, full of love. Often you will feel great pain in their presence as they pull from you all the dark energy that you can't see because you dwell within it. They will help all beings that take time to be with them,' said Fuff. 'I will look for a place for us to sleep this coming dark time whilst you look around for a place to dig a burrow.'

Rahh looked up into the arms of the great and ancient healers. He looked at how their fingers reached out and imagined how the green cloak would look when it came forth soon. He tried to feel what it would be like to live beneath such a great cloak, and thought perhaps he could even help the healers in their work or learn from them.

He hopped gently upon the earth stopping now and then to twitch his whiskers and look up into the arms that stretched in every direction. Eventually, he came to one particular healer who was very old and he felt its presence watching him. He sat for a while looking up at this great and ancient tree, seeing how it reached up carefully into the blue and how there seemed to be room around it as if the smaller healers and bushes honoured its space.

He continued to sit and then he began to ask through his heart if he would be welcome to build a home within the roots. He sat for a long while until he felt the Great Light falling lower in the blue but no answer had been given yet. It had been a long day and he thought that soon he had better look for Fuff and find a place to sleep before the dark time came.

He thanked the wise old healer and hopped away thinking to himself that he would continue to search tomorrow.

Fuff had already found a place for them for the night. He was twittering quietly in the bush when Rahh came along. 'Ah, Rahh,' he said. 'Did you find anywhere for your burrow?'

'Not exactly,' said Rahh, 'but I did find a wise old healer who had wonderful roots groaning over the surface of Mother and going deep into her. I asked him if I might dwell within his roots but he did not answer me. I sat for a while until I felt that it was time to come and find you.'

'Well, tomorrow is another day. We are in no hurry. This feels like a good place to stay for a while,' said Fuff.

'Yes indeed, it feels like we are being welcomed and it is a little warmer here too,' said Rahh.

Fuff replied, 'It is certainly warmer as we don't feel the winds blowing over the fields where there is no protection. Let us settle here. There is already a cosy place beneath this bush for you, Rahh, and I can sleep just above you in the tightly knit branches.'

Rahh snuffled the ground and scratched a soft bowl upon the earth to lie in. He lay on his back so that he could see Fuff above him.

'Ah, you are upside-down again,' said Fuff with a chuckle.

'Yes, this is so that I can see you whilst we speak,' said Rahh.

'Ah, do we have speaking to do then, Rahh?'

'Well, yes, I wanted to ask a question,' said Rahh. 'During the last cycle of the Great Light, especially when it all turned red, it was the most dramatic time that I have ever experienced. I do not think I have quite recovered from seeing you become a dragon, Fuff. The fire was terrifying.'

'Yes, that is why Red Fox covered his eyes, his fear was so great that he could not bear to look at you, Rahh,' said Fuff.

'Yes,' said Rahh, thoughtfully. 'The red sign on your feathers, Fuff. Was that always there?'

'No, it came slowly once I had begun to speak with the Dragon Fire upon my breath. But you have to be careful with such power. It can infect you and it can make you behave in a rough and unkind way. You have to learn how to control it, like trying to control the flying dragon each time it comes,' said Fuff.

'Does it come often?' asked Rahh.

'Not at first. It comes slowly so that you have time to play with it and learn. I think this is the first time it was given to you, Rahh, so that you could see the effect it had on Red Fox.'

'To play with?' said Rahh in alarm. 'I did not think it was a toy to play with.'

'That is how Mother and Father teach you how to Become. They give you power to play with and almost all creatures make errors with it because it makes you bigger than you are and then you make a fool out of yourself. But soon enough you learn how to control the power. And then something else happens,' said Fuff.

'What happens then?' asked Rahh, still with some alarm in his voice.

'As soon as you learn how to use the power correctly and appropriately and with reverence and respect for the source that gave it to you, then they give you more.' And Fuff chuckled to himself. 'Then you go through the whole game again, learning how to control the next measure of power and so it goes on until you become the Greatness of Everything itself.'

Rahh's eyes were wide with a hundred questions about the Dragon Fire. He was not sure that he ever wanted to feel it in his mouth again, let alone have more of it.

'Rahh, do not worry. Mother and Father are gentle with you. You will not make big mistakes if you trust them. But they want to bring power into the animals of the wood for then they can do good things with it,' said Fuff.

'Such as what?' asked Rahh.

'Such as help others to learn the wisdom of the healers. There is much healing to be done throughout the kingdom of the forest. There is sickness and disease in the minds of some animals, because they did not learn how to walk the Path of Life through the forest in a right and balanced way,' Fuff replied.

'Helping others seems like something that I might like to learn,' mused Rahh. 'But how does turning into a dragon help others? Surely it terrifies them!'

[183]

'The dragon is a wonderful creature, Rahh. Do not forget that I am the dragon as well as how you see me now. And you are not afraid of me as I am now. The power of the dragon can be brought to many situations for helping because it is a great fiery power. For example, once in a while one of the great healers will crash to the woodland floor. It can be a terrifying sound and the ground shakes like the Mother is coming through with all the dragons from the underworld. It has been known for a healer to fall upon the nests or burrows of little homes and the power of the dragon can be brought to lift the fallen healer and save the small creatures beneath,' said Fuff.

'More than that,' continued Fuff. 'The fire is transformational. It can be breathed into the hearts of creatures that hope for inner change – but that is a long story and for another day.'

'Will I actually turn into a dragon as you did, Fuff?' asked Rahh.

'Yes, you will Rahh. It will not be for a long time yet though. First the Mother will bring the fire to you, a little at a time so that you learn how to feel it and then control it. Next, you will be able to call upon it and bring it yourself. Thirdly, you will develop a red patch on the front of your fur, which will be the sign that you are a keeper of the Dragon Fire and it lives within you. Once that begins to grow upon you soon after you will have your first full dragon experience,' said Fuff.

Rahh was quite terrified by this and was very quiet, thinking about his fear.

'I see your fear,' said Fuff.

'Oh yes, I had forgotten again that you can see my thoughts,' said Rahh.

'You must not worry, Rahh. It is a natural part of your growth. Did you worry after the Dragon Fire came out of your mouth and terrified Red Fox?'

'No, I was just confused,' said Rahh.

'Well, it will be the same on your first transformation into the dragon. It will be a natural step for you because Mother and Father will have prepared you for it. When it comes, you will not expect it and also it will not come in any way that you can possibly imagine,' said Fuff. 'Does it worry you to rise into the blue Rahh?'

'No. Actually I was in the blue once before,' Rahh answered.

'You were in the blue, like a dragon?' asked Fuff, surprised.

'Yes, my friend Zzard took me beneath his body and into the blue when we were looking for Golden Rabbit. But it was only the once. It was strange to be without weight and moving through the invisibility and over the tops of the healers,' said Rahh.

'Really, what a great experience Rahh!' said Fuff. 'You are indeed a great rabbit!'

'Now, I think that I must sleep Rahh. Already the heavens are shining and the woodland is very peaceful. Shall we rest?'

'Yes, I too am ready. It has been a lovely day, Fuff. I am very happy that we have shared it together, and I am looking forward to the next rising of the Great Light where we might continue our journey,' said Rahh.

'Yes, and I. Sleep in peace, Rahh.'

'Yes, thank you. Sleep in peace, Fuff.'

The woodland creatures soon fell into slumber and indeed peace was all around, for these were special creatures – carrying both the Light of Father and the Fire of Mother into our world.

42

The Wind Spirit

Rahh and Fuff drifted into peaceful slumber beneath the sparkling heavens. The air was still cool as the green cloaks had not yet come forth from the arms of the healers.

As the dark time drew on Rahh began to stir in his sleep. He turned over, his feet wriggled, his ears were hot and eventually he awoke.

'What is it?' he said to himself. 'What is it that is waking me?'

His whiskers were moving by themselves. A breeze was floating gently through the wood and it began to come under the bush where Rahh was now awake and listening. The breeze turned into a gentle warm wind, blowing through the cold night air... and then Rahh heard a voice.

'RRRaaahhhhhhhh,' spoke the wind in a gentle whisper.

'RRRaaahhhhhhhh,' it came again.

The warmth and sound were so gentle that Rahh thought that he was back in the dreamtime but then it came a little stronger and he stirred to look out from under the bush.

'What is it? Who is that,' he whispered.

'It is I,' said the voice.

'Yes, but who are you?' whispered Rahh again.

'I am the spirit that blows through every life within the forest,' it answered.

'What do you want? Erm... I mean, how can I help you?' asked Rahh.

'I have blown this way since before the Great Light rose into the blue for the very first time, RRRaaahhhhhhhh. I have followed your life and at times I have guided your steps. Each time you breathe you feel my presence in your centre and when I blow cold, you shiver. Once, I lifted you into the invisibility beneath the Zzard's great feathers; and once I breathed life upon you when you were close to the long rabbit sleep,' said the voice of the wind spirit.

'I come with a message of welcome. You are welcome in this old and ancient woodland. It is a place full of the wisdom of trees,' it continued.

'You call them healers. They are the wisdom keepers of Mother Earth. They connect the heavenly father with the Earthly Mother. They grow from her bosom and reach up to Father Heaven to receive his light. They act as a bridge between Heaven and Earth, such is their great wisdom,' said the wind spirit.

'They are the wisdom keepers of the ages and they live in great peace. Only those with a golden heart can receive their wisdom.'

'Ohhh,' said Rahh, not really knowing what else to say.

'The trees do not move. They are rooted to the spot but I am their messenger, for I can blow anywhere. The wisdom keepers send you a message. They say, thank you.'

'Thank me for what? I did not do anything!' said the little rabbit.

'It is not what you do but what you are and how you became it,' said the wind spirit. 'You already did more in this life than many do in one hundred lives. You are a great rabbit, Rahh, and your work has been acknowledged.'

'After the dark time awaken early before the Great Light brightens the blue and walk to the wisdom keeper that you spoke with today. Then wait and wait and wait until you know that you need not wait any longer,' said the wind spirit.

As Rahh was thinking how to find the healer again the temperature cooled and the wind spirit had gone, leaving peace and silence behind her.

He crept back into his bed and was quite comfortable from the warm wind. He lay restfully in the silence of the dark time, listening to the stillness and peace in the wood. He could hear Fuff breathing above him still fast asleep and he thought to himself, 'My life is blessed.'

43

The Keys to the Green Kingdoms

Rahh knew that something had woken him but didn't know what it was. His eyes were wide open and he crept out quietly so as not to wake Fuff.

He hopped a little then stopped; sensed all around with his whiskers and hopped a little more. It was as if he had to keep stopping to hear the silence and peace in the wood. Soon he had found the great healer he was with during the last cycle of the Great Light. It became clear to him now that this old tree was indeed a wisdom keeper full of knowledge, and he sat and looked up at it for a while. He then hopped around it and decided to sit where he had done previously when asking if he could make his burrow here.

Well, he sat and he sat and he sat. Fuff's music started to the east of him somewhere distant in the wood and the Great Light began to brighten the arms and fingers of the healers.

Rahh was very patient. He felt warm and loved and even the earth felt different here. Welcoming is how he would put it, he thought. The invisibility was now full of music from many of the feathered creatures and the shadows were shortening as the Great Light rose higher.

Rahh began to think that perhaps the wind spirit had made a mistake and wondered how long he must wait. Then the sound of a word came out of nowhere: 'Patience.'

'Oh,' thought Rahh, 'where did that sound come from?'

He looked up and down and all around him and saw no other creatures. Then he began to wonder if he had just made it up in his head but he continued to sit with his ears alert and his whiskers twitching now and then.

As he looked down at his feet he could see the earth was cracked and dry. His eyes wandered along the crack until it reached the trunk of the great healer. He felt that he should follow it so he got up and hopped slowly along the crack in the earth until he reached the trunk of the tree.

'Mmm, it doesn't go any further,' he said to himself.

Then the voice came again, 'Then you have no vision,' it said.

Rahh definitely heard it this time. It was not his imagination and it was quite loud. He hopped back to where he had been sitting all morning. He turned and looked up to see where the voice came from but there were no other creatures visible. He was in a good position and could see all around him, he looked right and left and pointed his ears in all directions.

Suddenly there was a great blast of very hot wind. The arms of the healer swooped low enclosing the rabbit in its fingers. Rahh was lifted from the ground a little and then placed down gently again next to the trunk of the tree.

'Tell me what you see,' said the deep voice.

Rahh looked around. He could see the silvery grey of the trunk, the crack in the ground and the earth itself but nothing else.

'Look at me and look with your heart.'

'Who are you, and *where* are you?' asked Rahh, not knowing at all where this voice was coming from.

The hot wind again blew the arms of the healer wildly and Rahh lay down quickly so as not to be knocked off his feet.

'In a moment I will lift you again into the blue and shake your vision awake,' said the voice with some impatience.

Rahh was confused, but that was not unusual and he thought the voice must be coming from this great healer. He began to concentrate hard, looking at the trunk.

'Do not concentrate with your mind but relax and look with your heart,' said the deep voice.

Rahh tried to relax and his mind began to drift and think

about how lovely this place was; he could feel the warmth of the Great Light coming through the woodland and suddenly he saw through the tree. The trunk was not there but in its place was a shimmering doorway of many layers of green. He could even see through the doorway and beyond it.

'These are my green kingdoms,' the voice stated.

'Who are you,' asked Rahh?

'I am The All,' came the reply.

'What is The All?' Rahh asked.

'I am the Greatness of Everything. I am the Great Mystery. I am all you can ever know and more than that; and I am the unknowable. There is nothing you can do or say that can describe me. I am merely The All and at the same time I am nothing.'

Well, that description did nothing for Rahh's confusion, which was like some kind of circular game inside his head.

'But where are you?' asked Rahh. 'I hear your voice but I do not see you.'

'I am in the wind spirit, I am in the invisibility, I am the spirit of the tree and I am within the music that fills your ears. I am everywhere and I am awakening within your heart. That is where you hear me,' said The All.

'Now your heart has opened you can see into the truth of this tree. Indeed, it is full of the wisdom of the ages. Indeed, it is a great healer of all things that live and have a heart. Your heart is now a key to open my green kingdoms,' said The All.

'Today Rahh, through your courage to follow the guidance of the wind spirit and your patience, you have been given the Keys to the Green Kingdoms. With patience and love in your heart, you can now unlock any door and enter therein. Can you see the shimmering layers of green?' it continued.

'Yes,' said Rahh.

'That is love, and only a gentle, open heart has the key to enter it,' said The All.

'Thank you,' said Rahh. The words tumbled through his

whiskers seeming to overrule his mind and his desire to ask more questions.

'You are welcome, Rahh. This place welcomes you. You are of the spirit of all things that become love so look carefully and you can make your new home in this place, which is of the green shimmering veils of love,' said The All.

Rahh seemed to know that the speaking was finished. He sat for a moment and hopped back to the place he had been sitting since before the Great Light rose. He looked up at the tree but still it didn't say anything; however he noticed that he could still see through parts of it and hopped towards the vision of where there seemed to be a doorway in the trunk.

Sitting on the dry earth between two great roots he peered through the doorway into a wonderful place of moving shimmering veils, iridescent and shining, like the wings of a flitterflind. As he gazed in wonderment he felt the ground moving beneath him.

Untroubled by this movement he looked down and saw the earth was opening before his feet. But suddenly, thinking he was going to fall into the earth, Rahh leapt into the air in panic and came down upon a strong root. As the earth continued tumbling into the hole, Fuff suddenly appeared next to him in a flash and a flurry of reds and browns.

'Ahhh, you startled me Fuff!' the little rabbit exclaimed. 'Be careful! The earth is falling in.'

'I see that you have learned how to command the Mother to create a burrow for you,' said Fuff, laughing at Rahh's panic, fear and confusion.

'I did not do anything,' said Rahh. 'The earth shook and then there was this big hole.'

'Oh, I see,' said Fuff. 'Well, you are the rabbit. I think you should go down the hole and investigate.'

'I am not sure. What if it all falls in on me?'

'You will be able to dig your way out again. After all, you are a rabbit, a powerful digger,' Fuff replied.

'But I have never dug a burrow or indeed dug myself out of one,' said Rahh.

This conversation of reason and objection went on for quite some time and eventually Fuff said, 'Rahh, are we going to stand here all day or are you going to have a look down this hole?'

Rahh realised that he couldn't make any more excuses. He felt that his courage had gone but indeed this hole had opened up right at his feet and so perhaps it was meant for him, as Fuff had said some time ago.

'Very well, I will peep in and see what I can see,' said Rahh.

Rahh stepped towards the hole and Fuff was tempted to push him down it but he could feel the rabbit fear in Rahh. He looked towards the healer shaking his head from side to side in mock despair.

'This is the great rabbit. The one that terrified Red Fox with the Dragon Fire. The rabbit who flew through the invisibility beneath the great feathers of Zzard; and now he is afraid of going down a little hole, which rabbits do every day,' said Fuff under his breath.

Rahh poked his head into the hole and took another step forward then finally disappeared completely. Fuff fluttered upwards and sat in the arms of the healer, making a little music to amuse himself and entertain the woodland. After some time Fuff began to wonder where Rahh had gone to. He flew down and looked into the hole.

'Rahhhh!' he shouted. 'Are you in there?'

There was no reply so Fuff poked his head into the hole and shouted again.

'Rahhhh, are you in there?'

Still there was no reply, but the hole looked fine and very deep. 'Perhaps Rahh is exploring,' thought Fuff. 'Well, I'll go and eat something and come back shortly,' he said to himself. As he was about to leave there was a great sound of creaking and heaving and the roots of the healer began to move. They closed together where the entrance to the hole was and then the entrance was completely gone.

'Oh my word,' said Fuff, and flew up into the arms of the healer, whistling and twittering loudly in alarm.

'HELP! My friend is down that hole,' he shouted. 'What are you doing? You have locked my friend beneath the ground.' He flew down again shouting, 'Rahh, Rahh where are you?'

Meanwhile, Rahh came up the track from where he had slept during the last dark time to see Fuff dancing wildly and throwing bits of earth aside with his beak. 'What are you doing, Fuff?' he asked.

Fuff shot round to look at Rahh. 'How did you get out of the earth?' he asked. 'I was terribly worried. Look, the roots of the tree closed together and the hole disappeared. How did you get out?'

'I will show you,' said Rahh, 'but you must come with me into the hole first.'

'But there is no hole, Rahh. It has closed up,' said Fuff.

'The hole will be there in a moment,' said Rahh.

'But, I can't go into a hole. I am a creature of the invisibility, not the dark underground world,' said Fuff, making as many objections as he could.

'You must come, Fuff. It is a great part of your learning.'

'Oh, so now you are the teacher and I am the student,' said Fuff looking indignantly at Rahh.

Rahh laughed. 'Well you might look at it that way,' he said, 'because I know something that you don't. And if you wish to know it too then you will have to enter the hole. Now, watch the earth,' said Rahh. He stepped towards the tree and sat on the root then looked up at the trunk of the tree and the roots parted and the hole appeared.

[194]

'What is happening? How did that happen?' said Fuff, hopping up and down and spinning in circles.

'You asked me not long ago if I had learned to command the Mother into making a burrow for me. Well, the answer is very similar,' said Rahh. 'Last night as you slept, I was visited by the wind spirit.'

'The wind spirit?' repeated Fuff in amazement.

'Yes,' said Rahh. 'She was warm and tender and told me to come here before the Great Light rose and wait for an answer to my question about digging a burrow here. I waited and waited and nothing happened and then a voice spoke to me. It showed me a doorway through the trunk of the tree but really it wasn't a door, it was a vision of beauty where the great trunk of the tree should be. But at the same time it was a doorway into the green kingdoms. I was given the keys to the green kingdoms in my heart, and now I can open any door,' he concluded.

'But only The All can give you the keys to the green kingdoms!' said Fuff.

'Yes, that is who the voice said that he was.'

'The voice, Rahh? But do you know what this means?'

'Yes, I can open any door into the green kingdoms,' Rahh replied. 'And it appears that I can command holes to appear in the earth, too.'

'No, Rahh. Well, I mean yes, Rahh, but it also means that the voice of The All has spoken in your heart,' said Fuff. 'That is the most wonderful and amazing thing and shows to me that you have been chosen.'

'What does chosen mean?' asked Rahh.

'It means so much that I cannot even begin to tell you,' said Fuff.

'But you already told me that Mother had chosen me when I was given the Dragon Fire,' puzzled Rahh.

'Yes, Rahh, but this is different. This means that you have been chosen by The All, which goes beyond any description. Even I do not know the wisdom of The All. No other creature in the wood has ever been chosen this way – I have no idea where to begin. If this is so, then you are now the teacher and I must become the humble student, Rahh, for The All has yet to speak through my heart. I must now bow down to you and honour you as my teacher. I am so blessed to have received you into my life,' said Fuff.

'Don't be silly, Fuff, I am just a rabbit,' Rahh laughed. 'Now, are you coming down this hole?'

'Yes Master. If you wish me to enter into the dark underground world with you then I will do whatever you wish. I must have misjudged how much wisdom you have. Please forgive me, Master,' said Fuff.

Laughing to himself at the absurdity of this role reversal that Fuff was now engineering, Rahh said, 'Follow me. We don't have time for this game of student and teacher.' And he turned and hopped down the hole into the blackness of Mother Earth's embrace. Fuff followed quickly on his tail, somewhat in trepidation, being a creature of the invisibility.

44

Down the Rabbit Hole

The hole seemed very deep to Fuff never having been underground before. He kept his beak on Rahh's tail so as not to get lost in the darkness. Then he noticed that actually it wasn't that dark.

'Rahh, it is not completely dark down here,' he remarked.

Rahh stopped and turned around. 'Yes, that's right Fuff. What can you see?'

'Well, I can't see clearly, like under the Great Light but there is a kind of glow,' said Fuff.

'What colour is the glow?' Rahh asked.

'I am not sure,' said Fuff.

'Wait here and I will move down the burrow a little and then see if you can determine any colours,' said Rahh. He hopped a little way further on and Fuff stayed where he was. 'Yes, I think there is a slight green glow and I can still see you,' he said.

'Very good, then let us go a little deeper into the earth,' said Rahh.

Fuff hopped along the burrow catching up with Rahh and the two continued down into the earth. Presently the burrow opened up into a chamber with fresh grass for bedding. The green glow was slightly brighter here and Rahh stopped and turned to Fuff. 'Are you still afraid of being in the burrow?' he asked.

'No, not at all. It is very pleasant and warm and you have fresh grass as a bed too. How did this come to be here, Rahh?'

'It is like the gifts that the animals left in the woodland. It was given to me in gratitude. It was all prepared for me as I needed it, and then it was given,' the rabbit replied.

'Who gave it to you? Who dug the burrow and laid the bedding?' asked Fuff.

'Who do you think would know what a rabbit needs?' questioned Rahh in return.

'Perhaps another rabbit?'

Rahh laughed and said to Fuff that this was indeed a very wise answer, then continued.

'Make yourself comfortable, and I will tell you,' said Rahh.

'Thank you, Master,' said Fuff, feeling that he was again the student.

Rahh chuckled. 'I am not your master, Fuff. I am just a rabbit. I am sure that we both know things that the other does not. This does not make us master and student, but allows us to share our knowledge and help the other to grow.'

Fuff was thinking that suddenly everything was quite bizarre and unusual. Here he was, a creature used to sailing through the invisibility, down a hole with a strange green glow and a Master rabbit. Yet he was already comfortable in this strange underground world that only a short time before had terrified him.

'What do you remember about the colour green, Fuff?' asked Rahh.

'It is the colour of love,' said Fuff. 'Our mother's love.'

'So, where do you think the green glow comes from?' asked Rahh. 'Think about where we are.'

'We are under the ground, which should be terrifying for a creature of the invisibility like me,' said Fuff. 'But I am not afraid any longer. In fact, I could even be a rabbit as this is a very pleasant place to be.'

'So, if we are underground, where are we?' asked Rahh again.

Fuff tried to spin into a fluttering flap and disappear up into the arms of the healers, which is what he always did when challenged to find an answer to something that he didn't know. But this time he hit his head on the roof of the burrow and fell back in a crumpled heap of red and brown feathers.

'There is no escape,' said Rahh, laughing at his friend. 'You can't just rise into the blue as a way of getting out of learning the answers. Relax and I will tell you. When you are in the earth, you are in the heart of Mother's love. All around you is love. The green glow is the warmth from her heart and she guides our way through the darkness as she feels our need,' he explained.

'Oh,' said Fuff, feeling confused and thinking to himself that this must be what a rabbit feels like most of the time. 'So, did the Mother provide this burrow for you?'

'You asked me who would know what a rabbit needs,' said Rahh. 'Well, both Mother and Father know what a rabbit needs. Mother provides the practical things of the physical world and Father teaches us how to ask for it.'

'Oh,' said Fuff again, not knowing what else to say.

'Father asked the great healer to open up a space for me by moving his strong and powerful roots. Then the healer carried a message from Father to Mother asking to give the burrow warmth and light.'

'Why did Father not ask Mother directly?' asked Fuff.

'Because he only speaks to her through the heart of one who dwells alongside her. One who is a bridge between Heaven and Earth,' Rahh replied. 'The healers are bridges between Heaven and Earth and so Father and Mother can communicate directly through the open heart of the healer or through the open heart of any creature. Sometimes Father or Mother speak into the heart of an individual, guiding them and giving them ideas. When the creature begins to work with the idea or share this information with others, then the energy of mother or the light of Father is passed on and the flow then continues,' said Rahh.

'In this way, Father and Mother give the individual an opportunity to learn how to be a creator and to join in the great game of creation. When they do this their hearts begin to open more,' he explained.

'How do you know all these things?' asked Fuff.

'I don't know. I can't tell you. It just comes to me now and then when someone needs to know. I feel Father and Mother speaking through me to bring the answers to those who truly want to know the truth,' said Rahh.

'But how did you arrive behind me earlier after the earth closed up?' asked Fuff.

'Mother dug the burrow all the way to the place where I slept under the bush during the last dark time. She showed me that I can have a burrow as long and deep as I like. So, I came out of the earth in my bed,' said Rahh, with his whiskers twitching to show how clever he was.

'And what about the keys to the green kingdoms? What do they do,' asked Fuff.

'The keys to the green kingdoms allow your heart to open any door into the nature spirit worlds and this allows you to learn how to communicate with the spirits of the healers and other beings of the woodlands and Earth. Once you open those doors, the spirits will often help you to dig a burrow too or create anything you need such as food,' said Rahh.

'Master you are truly a great rabbit to know all these things about heaven and earth and to also have the keys to the green kingdoms. May I be your student?' asked Fuff.

'Fuff, I am sure it is now late and the Great Light is already resting his head, so I think it is time that we found our places to sleep for the night or we will be tired tomorrow.'

'Yes, Master, you are right. I have more than enough new ideas in my head to keep me awake for many dark times with worry and wonder,' said Fuff.

'Would you like to sleep in this burrow with me for this first night, Fuff?' asked Rahh.

'Yes, indeed, it is so warm and cosy in here. I might even like to sleep here on regular occasions,' said Fuff.

'And so may that be, if you so desire it,' said Rahh.

Rahh and Fuff fluffed up the grass for their beds. Fuff made a little nest of grass and Rahh created a nice soft pillow for his head on the other side of the chamber.

'Are you comfortable, Fuff,' asked Rahh?

'Yes, I am very warm and cosy, thank you.'

The green glow faded slowly into the background and warmth seemed to rise through the earth. The creatures were indeed very warm and cosy and were soon sleeping in extreme peacefulness, held in the loving embrace of Mother.

45

The Sweet Life

Rahh felt the rising of the Great Light as his fire bathed the face of Mother Earth. He popped out of the burrow beneath the arms of the great healer and flicked his whiskers at the blue. Fuff was already making music in the distance and Rahh could hear him moving about and exploring this new woodland.

Rahh was ready for some fine breakfast grass and set off to find a glade that was lit by the Great Light in the blue. This morning he was really ready for a Light breakfast. He needed to feel Mother's bright jewels in his belly, so off he went.

Fuff would find him soon enough and they would eat together and then sit around and talk then rest a while before eating again and then bed.

As the days unfolded the two friends shared many stories and made a happy life for themselves in this ancient wood. Fuff would flit and flee to new places and call to Rahh to come and look. Rahh would hop here and there following Fuff's calls and when he caught up with him they would explore together.

Presently the buds burst and the great green cloak unfolded from the arms of the healers and the colour of love was everywhere. The Great Light hung longer in the blue until it was time for it once again to bathe another part of Mother Earth and the days grew shorter again. They were happy times and it seemed to Rahh that they had been together as friends forever.

Word spread through the woodland that the Dragon Rabbit lived here and that Red Fox would never, ever be seen again. Many small creatures came to live in this peaceful place. Some would come and peep through the grass to take a look at this great and courageous rabbit. Small creatures even dared to come out at night and forage, making small nests and burrows knowing that they would not be eaten by any animals of the dark time.

Eventually, the Great Cycle of Light shortened and the green cloak had turned to reds, golds and browns. Rahh and Fuff knew that the healers would soon call to sister wind to lay their rich colours upon the earth in the celebration of transformation. The friends watched daily as the arms of the healers became bare once more and the invisibility in the dark time became cold.

When it was very cold Fuff would sleep in the burrow with Rahh, but essentially, he was a creature of the invisibility and so he couldn't spend too many nights in the burrow. But he was very happy to have a choice of a different kind of bed to give his thin legs a rest from sitting on twigs all through the dark time.

Soon, the Great Light had almost disappeared to the south and Rahh felt the chill of the white lands upon his whiskers. It was time to store a little food in the burrow, even though he still had plenty from the gifts of the woodland creatures.

Rahh and Fuff spoke about preparations and Rahh made a new warm place for Fuff in case he wanted to spend more time in the burrow. However, Fuff was still enthusiastic flitting and flapping here and there but more briskly when it was chilly.

The blue began to turn grey and the green cloaks of the healers had finished their colourful celebrations and fallen to the earth to keep the roots warm. Fuff and Rahh sat quietly by the bush where they had spent their first night in the new woodland. It was a favourite place that they returned to often. Rahh would get into his old bed beneath the bush and Fuff would flap and fizz into the fingers of the bush above Rahh's head.

They had a special time here for they would lie together and look at the pinpoints of light in the heaven and wonder about how there could be such powerful beauty all around.

The cycle of warmth had passed and Rahh had grown a thick coat against the white lands that were coming. They would not be able to lie out and watch the heavens much longer and so this was a good time to be together.

The invisibility was falling upon them in cold waves and Rahh became restless for his warm burrow. Fuff wanted to stay in the bush this dark time and so the friends bid each other a good night and Rahh went down the hole beneath the bush towards his comfortable chamber within the earth.

The time for singing and making music was over as the dark time came, but Fuff was captivated by the beauty of the naked woodland beneath the heavens. However, he was aware of the east wind coming too, which brought the bitterness with it. He nestled deep into the bush and was soon asleep peacefully.

Rahh was also soon sleeping in the warmth of Mother's embrace and all of the woodland creatures were very still. They were all preparing for the cold to come.

The dark time deepened and the ground began to swim with movement from the east wind building up. Rahh became restless, turning in his bed and twitching his whiskers. A shiver ran through him and he awoke. Laying still he listened with all of his body to the Earth and everything in the woodland. He could feel so much these days. He had become so sensitive to all life and he was greatly awakened when any kind of change was coming.

As he lay sensing the woodland a warm wind began to blow through his burrow.

'RRRaaahhhhhh,' came a warm, whispering voice.

Rahh knew it immediately as the spirit of the wind who had helped him find this burrow. His ears went up and his whiskers twitched.

'Greetings, blessed spirit. I hear you,' he said.

'RRRaaahhhhhh, bitterness is coming. The east wind blows and changes are on their way. Keep warm and stay safe for there is much for you to do.'

The spirit of the wind blew through his fur and warmed him.

He put his chin on the earth and as he wondered about her words he slipped away into the rabbit dreamtime.

As he slept he drifted into a vision. A great wave of water came tumbling down the burrow and washed him out through the roots of the great healer. He lay bedraggled on the ground, his fur soaked. He looked to the healer for help, as once it had bent forward and lifted him from the earth but help did not come this time.

The tree's spirit looked at Rahh and said, 'Stay warm and safe, Rahh, for changes are coming.'

Rahh could hear more water roaring through the burrow and suddenly it burst out of the hole in a great explosion, washing him away and down the hill towards the edge of the wood. He could not hold his ground. He had no control any longer and he feared for losing his life. The water carried him at great speed out of the wood and towards the pool where first he had seen the Great Light turn red just before the dragon flew over his head.

He could see the red fire of the dragon coming out of the pool and he couldn't stop himself. Just as he was going to be washed into the fiery waters he awoke from the dreamtime with a start. He was wet with sweat and felt the rabbit fear coming upon him before he realised that he had been in the dreamtime. He calmed himself a little. He was breathing heavily and full of terror as he realised that he could still hear the roaring of the water.

Fear turned to panic and his ears shot upright. 'What is that sound? Is water coming down the burrow?' he thought.

He struggled to come out of his dream and was not really sure what was happening. He tucked his head down again and shuffled up against the wall to feel safe. The roaring was getting louder, but he could not smell water.

'Where is my courage,' he thought. 'I am full of fear again but I must go to the entrance of the burrow and see what is happening.'

Upon that thought the earth shuddered with a great thundering crash and a huge cry rent the whole woodland. All the spirits of the green kingdoms were in pain.

Suddenly, Rahh felt the lion coming from his heart and he got to his feet and ran up the burrow to the entrance. Now, he knew what the roaring sound was. It was the east wind ripping through the woodland with great anger.

Something had upset her and she was blowing like he had never seen or heard before. He popped his head out of the burrow and another great crashing sound hurtled through the healers. It was an arm, ripped from a tree nearby. The ground looked like the waves of a great ocean, heaving in a swell of browns and bronzes as the leaves swam in all directions in terror.

Rahh suddenly thought of Fuff and dashed back down the burrow, through the tunnels, past the sleeping chamber and towards his other bed beneath the bush where Fuff was sleeping. As he approached the exit of the burrow the whole woodland was moving above him and the bush was no longer there. It had been torn away from its roots.

Rahh was quite frightened again and wondered where his lion had gone when he needed it. He was seeing and feeling things that he had never experienced before. He was afraid to put his head out of the burrow as so many things were being driven across the earth by the anger of the east wind.

Rahh got as close as he dared to the exit of the burrow and began to shout Fuff's name. But his voice was completely drowned out by the noise of the wind and all the debris of the woodland flying past the burrow entrance.

He turned and ran back through the burrow to the entrance between the roots of the great healer.

'Tree spirit, can you hear me,' he shouted.

A deep but gentle voice came back to him. 'Rahh, go to your bed where you are safe. There is nothing you can do out here until the east wind passes. Go to your bed and be safe. Do as I bid now, quickly,' said the healer.

'Have you seen Fuff?' he shouted again.

'Go NOW,' roared the healer in a growl that alarmed and frightened Rahh such was its power. Even before he could move another great thundering crash shook the earth just behind his head. He bolted down the hole and into his sleeping chamber where he pulled up the dry grass around him and lay close to the wall for safety.

Rahh began to shake with fear. He put his nose between his paws and his whiskers curled downwards. He closed his eyes and tears began to run down his fur. He felt his world was changing. He felt helpless, cold and hungry. Even the light of love in the burrow had gone to sleep.

Rahh felt a feeling that he had not felt for many, many cycles of the Great Light.

He felt alone.

46

Changes

The east wind roared, howled and screamed like a pack of giant invisible creatures flying through the wood. The Great Light rose and fell three times before the tail of the beast passed and all began to calm.

Rahh had lain in his chamber unable to move, not so much from fear now as he had got used to the dreadful sounds of the east wind and what it was doing above, but because he felt so helpless and empty. Empty, that is, except for the pain that he could feel above the ground. It was a pain that he did not know and it hurt him deeply.

He had tried to sleep through the storm as it seemed pointless to be awake but he couldn't stop wondering if Fuff had found shelter. The terrible noises quietened down other than for an eerie wailing sound, which he thought was the tail of the wind groaning through the arms of the healers. He thought, perhaps it was safe now to go to the burrow entrance and look out. Firstly, he hopped along the burrow to where his sleeping bush had stood but no light was coming in from the entrance. As he got closer he could see that the burrow had been filled with earth and leaves and was essentially sealed.

He retraced his steps, passing his chamber again and went to the main entrance. He could see the light at the end of the burrow, which cheered him a little and very gingerly he popped his head out.

'Oh my whiskers!' he exclaimed. 'Oh my whiskers, what has happened?'

Rahh saw what the great thundering crashes had been. All

around the great healers had been ripped from the ground and lay torn and smashed, perishing upon the earth. Now he knew that the pain he felt was the pain of the community each time a brother or sister tree had fallen. The wailing was from the tree spirits mourning the loss of those whose lives were slowly slipping away into the Earth. For a moment he felt his old heart-pain for the loss of Golden Rabbit.

Rahh's world had changed. Nothing was the same. The debris of a destroyed woodland lay all around him and other than the wailing of the trees there were no other sounds. The Great Light was behind a sheet of grey and there was no music to be heard.

All the pathways that Rahh had made to his favourite places were gone. Arms and fingers of the healers lay all around and the roof of the woodland had disappeared allowing the grey light to pour in. It was like he had emerged from his burrow into a new wood; a new world but one full of pain and devastation.

Rahh was overwhelmed with the feelings of grief from the healers. He felt full of them and did not know what his own feelings were anymore, such was the weight of pain in his body. But he suddenly thought that he should find some sweet breakfast grass and perhaps he would then feel better and be able to see things more clearly.

The path to his favourite breakfast glade was gone and so he picked his way carefully through and under the broken trees towards a bright area where the grey light was falling through the space where the woodland roof used to be.

Strangely, the morning grass was actually very sweet. It felt good in his tummy and he sensed that he was coming alive again. His mind began to clear and awaken and although he found it strange that he was not in fear at all from these changes, he was worried about Fuff. He sat up and his ears rose and flicked here and there listening. Then another thought came. 'Mmmm, when my belly is full then I will be in a good way to go and seek Fuff.'

As Rahh continued to eat he heard a rustling sound behind

him. The earth was moving, lifting upwards in a mound, and then a small nose appeared through the earth followed by a head. The head looked at Rahh and he looked at the head.

'Good morning,' said the head.

'Good morning,' said Rahh.

The head continued to come out of the ground followed by a velvety body then the small furry creature shook himself and looked back down the hole. 'All is safe,' he shouted and then some other similar but smaller creatures popped out into the open too.

Rahh sat and watched chewing on his breakfast. All in all five creatures came out of the hole and once they had all emerged the first one turned to Rahh again and spoke.

'Good morning again to you. Indeed it is a wonderful morning,' said the creature and continued to address Rahh. 'That was a fierce time beneath the earth. We have many places to lie and rest but all of them were crushed by the thundering crashes.'

'I am Rown from the field of the red mirror to the east and this is my family. We have been cut off from our routes and are a little lost. We need to dig some new pathways to return to our homeland. We spend most of our time in the earth but with all the upset we thought we would come out and see what is happening on the surface now that the woodland is becoming quiet again.'

Rown looked at Rahh and his family lined up alongside him. Rahh felt that it was his turn to speak.

'Oh yes, good morning again,' said Rahh bristling his whiskers to show that he was happy to see them. 'I am Rahh and I have just come up from the earth too after three cycles of the Great Light. Indeed, the sounds were terrible and the pain of the great healers hurts me deeply.'

'Yes,' said Rown, looking at his family. 'We could also feel this terrible pain above us but didn't know what it was.'

'Yes, many of their number have fallen and there is a deep sadness and wailing in the hearts of those who remain,' said Rahh.

Rown and his family could see how Rahh felt the pain. The

creature next to Rown stepped forward and looked into Rahh's eyes.

'I am Rowsen, wife of Rown,' she said. 'I see that the pain cuts deeply into you. Can we help you?'

Rahh was immediately touched by the beauty of her love and his pain burst from his heart in tears for all to see. He hadn't realised how deep it was. Rowsen looked round at the others and they all came and sat close to Rahh, each placing a small brown paw onto Rahh's which is the woodland way of bringing comfort.

'It is my friend, he is missing. I was just filling my empty tummy before going to look for him,' said Rahh. 'And I don't know what to do to help the healers; to help them with their pain of losing so many brothers and sisters. They pass into the other world so slowly and all around them have to watch helplessly as their light fades from this world.'

'Yes, it is always so painful when a healer falls to earth but there is a great wisdom within them and you need not worry. You will see that many new things will spring to fill their places. It will not be long before there is new life,' said Rowsen, and continued.

'We will help you,' and the other creatures nodded their agreement that they would help too. 'We have many connections in different places and we can spread the word that your friend is missing,' she said.

'But what about your own problems,' said Rahh. 'You have lost your way to your homeland.'

'We can spare time for you,' said Rown and the others nodded again.

'I know the fields to the east and the deep red pool that is a window into the Mother,' said Rahh. 'I was there many cycles ago for a great teaching from my friend.'

'Yes, we know of the pool and the legend that surrounds it. We have felt the earth tremble when the Great Light enters the pool,' said Rown. 'It is said that the Great Light comes down at certain times and the dragons of the earth fly out from the pool. We hear that the blue turns red and a great terror falls upon the earth,' he continued, looking at his family, who nodded in agreement, which seemed to be their way.

'It is the truth,' said Rahh. 'I have seen the dragon take to the blue with my own eyes and my missing friend knows the mystery of the Dragon Fire. His name is Fuff, a creature of the invisibility.'

More nodding of heads occurred from the small creatures indicating a kind of uncertainty.

Rahh detected their sudden fear of him because he knew of the Dragon Fire. 'There is nothing to fear. The Dragon Fire is given to those who are at one with the sacred heart of the Mother Earth. It is to help protect the innocent ones,' he said.

Rowsen leaned forward to speak. 'It is said in the legend that there is a great one who put the fear of the long sleep into Red Fox. So much so, that he ran from the wood never to return. Is this true also and was it the Dragon Fire that did this?'

'Yes, that is so. The legend is true. I know that this is a safe place from Red Fox. You are safe here,' said Rahh.

The small creatures all looked at each other feeling a little more at ease now.

Rahh said, 'You are creatures from beneath the earth but can you travel far upon the surface?'

'We are a little slow and cannot see very well but it is possible,' said Rown.

'Then perhaps I can lead you through the woodland to the eastern grasslands. It would not take long. We can rest along the way if needed,' said Rahh.

The creatures smiled and were joyful at this possibility. Rown said, 'There are many tunnels in the earth made by our ancestors but some of them were crushed in the great upheaval closing our way home. This would be a wonderful help if you can guide us.'

'Do you need to eat breakfast?' asked Rahh.

'No, we have not been short of food. We can go immediately,' said Rowsen, full of enthusiasm and looking at the others who were nodding their heads.

'Well, let me see. I have eaten breakfast for now. Yes, quite enough, Let me observe the Great Light for a moment.'

The Light had risen in the east and Rahh put it to his face where he felt its warmth through the greyness above, then said, 'Follow me and if I go too fast shout out and I will wait for you.'

The small velvety heads all nodded and the smaller creatures began to jump with excitement. Rahh began the journey, hopping towards the east then stopping to check that the small creatures were still behind him, which they were, smiling and travelling in a line one behind the other.

47

The Story

Rahh led the creatures into the east. It didn't take more than half a cycle of the Great Light and Rahh's tummy was certainly ready for luncheon grass as they arrived at the boundary of the woodland and the great eastern grasslands where the pool opened into the Mother's Heart. The small creatures were overjoyed to have arrived back in their homeland and gathered around Rahh.

'Thank you, Rahh. As we came out of the earth this morning we were lost and worried; but now, in such a short time it seems, we are home again and our hearts are filled with joy. Soon we will be once more beneath the great ocean of the green fields. We are so grateful. How can we thank you?' asked Rown.

'Your joy is my reward for helping you and hopefully you will carry it deep into the earth and share it with others to uplift all whom you meet,' Rahh replied.

Then Rowsen spoke. 'But Rahh, we offered to help you find your friend. Now we know the way shall we not come back with you and do just that?'

'Your joy fills me with hope and I am happy to travel back on my own for now. By the time I return the dark time will be upon us and I will take to my burrow until morning. I may even find my friend in the burrow as he sometimes pops in when the weather is difficult for him,' said Rahh.

'I see your pain is less than this morning Rahh, but it is replaced by another feeling,' said Rowsen.

'Yes, I have enjoyed helping you to find your homeland and as we walked and talked together a lot of my pain has indeed been taken from me by the healers that we passed along the way. But I also feel that other feeling,' said Rahh. 'It is uncertainty. The certainty that every morning would be filled with the golden music of Fuff is no longer there. The certainty that the wood will be filled with the green cloak of love in the next great cycle is no longer there and I feel there are many things I still don't understand about the great forest of life,' he went on.

Rowsen looked at her family and they all looked worried. 'How will you manage on your own,' she said. 'Is there anything we can do?'

'Yes,' said Rahh. 'There is something that you can do for me which would be a most wonderful thing.'

Rown stepped forward next to his wife and said, 'Please tell us, Rahh. We are so grateful to you for saving us that we will give anything that is in our power to give.' He looked at his family and they all nodded, which, as you know, was their way.

Rahh put his head low so that his chin was almost on the ground and level with the pretty faces of these velvety creatures, who couldn't see very well. 'When you go into the earth, into the ancient tunnels made by your ancestors, will you tell all whom you meet a story?'

Rown and Rowsen looked at each other and then at their children questioningly. 'Yes, of course,' said Rowsen, 'What story is this?'

'Will you tell them about these times of the great storm and the pain that was in the woodland and how you became lost,' said Rahh.

The velvety creatures all looked at each other again and nodded, feeling Rahh had more to say.

'And will you tell them how you came out into the wood and met a rabbit who helped you to find your way home?'

Rahh looked at them for their acknowledgement and they all nodded.

'And will you tell them that the rabbit told you the legends were true – and it is safe for all small creatures in this wood, because Red Fox dare not come here anymore?'

The creatures nodded again.

'And will you tell them that it was the Dragon Rabbit himself that led you home again?'

Rown put his head up questioningly and Rowsen signalled to her children to come closer. Rahh felt a wave of fear run through them.

'You are safe,' he said. 'You will always be safe here. I will show you. 'Sit quite still and I will run round you.'

He ran in three circles around the velvety creatures and the earth began to warm up beneath them. He stepped into the circle with them and said, 'Come close to my fur. Sit with me and watch.'

The grass that they sat upon was becoming warmer and a clear circle appeared on the ground. The circle grew bigger, pushing out from where they sat. The outer ring of the circle began to smoulder and smoke and then a loud crack rent the air, making them jump. By now their feet were very warm. Rahh bid them watch the circle closely and almost before his words had finished a fire of yellow flames burst through the earth upon the smoking circle. None of the creatures were afraid but Rown asked 'What is this?

'This is the Dragon Fire,' said Rahh.

'How does it come?' asked Rowsen.

'It comes at my command. I am the Dragon Rabbit that saved the wood from Red Fox and I am a carrier of the Dragon Fire. It is the love of Mother and nothing to be afraid of. From this day forward you will be able to tell this story and that there should be no fear of the Dragon Fire for it is gentle. Watch me,' said Rahh.

He hopped to the flames and passed his paw through them and said, 'Come, feel the fire of Mother.'

The creatures stepped forward and one by one they passed their paws through the yellow flames, which were cool to the touch. Rown fell upon Rahh's paws and cried, 'Thank you Great Rabbit for showing us this wonderful mystery. Truly your magic touches my heart in a deep way.' Rowsen put her paw on her husband to steady him and the children gathered round. Rown's tears spilled upon Rahh's paws and Rahh said, 'Today the light has touched your heart, Rown. You will grow as a great creature and others will wish to hear your story. As you walk out from this circle of fire you will change and the sign of love will be on your coat so that others will see that you speak the truth of this sacred day.'

At the end of Rahh's words the fire died down and disappeared. Rown turned to face his family who all gasped when they saw him.

'What is it?' he asked.

'It is the mark of the Dragon Fire upon your coat,' said Rowsen.

Rown looked down and saw that a patch of his fur had turned a reddish brown in colour. He looked questioningly at Rahh, who replied, 'It is the light from your heart, Rown. As the fire opened your heart, it showed its sign upon your coat. It will be with you forever to show the world that you have indeed witnessed the Dragon Fire of mother and seen that she is loving and safe. Tell this story well and all creatures who hear it will know that they are safe in this wood and these fields.'

'Each time you tell this story some of the fire in your heart will touch others and those whose tears come will be the ones whom Mother is blessing. All of you here will have the flowing waters soon. You will feel the love of Mother enter your hearts,' said Rahh.

The creatures were without words. It was like there was nothing to say any more. No words could describe how they felt. They were full of something that they didn't understand and their faces were filled with questions that they could not ask.

Rahh looked at them gently and said, 'What you feel is the power of love. It takes your words away, it takes your breath away and it burns holes in your heart. Once it comes then it will be with you forever. You have seen the love of Mother today and she has blessed you with her cool fire. Now go to find your tunnels and know that from this day forward they will be filled with Mother's love.'

Rowsen looked at her family. Rown was holding one paw on his heart, tears still flowing from his eyes.

'Can you find your way from here?' asked Rahh.

'Yes, indeed,' said Rowsen. 'Just to the north along the edge of the wood are some of the very old tunnels of our ancestors and we can soon burrow back into those and find our way.'

'You now have tunnels that lead deep into the woodland and if you need my help again you can perhaps open up those routes to find me,' said Rahh.

'Thank you, thank you, Rahh,' said Rowsen. 'Now that we know our directions again we will open the tunnels that were crushed by the falling healers deep into the woodland again. It will be a great adventure for us.'

She looked at the others and they all nodded in agreement and with some visible excitement that this would be a great task for them.

'It has been our great good fortune to have met you beneath the Great Light today,' said Rown.

Rowsen said, 'We will now spread the word beneath the ground that your friend Fuff is missing and that any news should be brought to us immediately and we will bring it to you through the woodland tunnels.'

'Thank you,' said Rahh, 'And now I must return home again.' Then he stopped and looked at the earth.

'What is it?' asked Rowsen.

'Suddenly, I had a feeling about the words that came from beneath my whiskers. I realised that I do not really have a home.

I just live where I am for now. Nothing is permanent for me but I am blown by the winds of fortune from one place to another and one experience to another in an ever-changing landscape of mystery and desire,' said Rahh.

'I feel a chill in the air, it cannot be long now before the white lands are upon us. Take to your tunnels and be warm and safe until the Great Light begins to rise high in the blue again. Perhaps we will see each other again before the Green Cloak brings forth its healing love and a new cycle to the woodland.'

Upon this sudden melancholy note, Rahh said goodbye. He was disturbed. He could feel that things were changing more than he thought earlier. He hopped into the woodland and looked back. The small creatures were scurrying north in a knowing way. Rahh was happy for them for indeed they were full of joy at being home again.

And full of love from the fire of Mother Earth.

48

The Celebration

Rahh was happy he had met the small creatures. They were warm and friendly and had promised to come to see him again when the cycle of the white lands had left and the warmth was returning.

As he wandered home through the wood his thoughts naturally turned to Fuff as he passed places where they had rested and talked together. There were also places where Rahh had even stopped to taste how sweet the grass was when they first arrived in this new wood. There were many memories of their journey together.

Rahh began to shout Fuff's name every now and then hoping to hear a reply or even some distant Fuff music, but all was quite silent after the visit of the strong east wind. The trees that remained standing were stripped bare and the debris of the east wind's anger was everywhere.

The Great Light was falling fast now and as Rahh approached his burrow he saw a gathering of creatures by the entrance. There were many different kinds of creature and as Rahh came closer one of their number stepped forward.

'Good evening,' said Rahh.

'Good evening, Lord,' said a brown creature with sparkling whiskers. Rahh thought he looked like a very large wood mouse with his long tail as he sat upon his haunches addressing him.

'I think you are mistaken! I am Rahh and this is the entrance to my burrow,' he said with his whiskers bristling upwards to let them know that he was friendly towards them.

'Great rabbit, you are our Lord. The Lord of this woodland

and the one who protects us against Red Fox and other dangers, and we are so grateful to have you dwell here amongst us. We are so blessed by your presence,' said the creature.

'Well, I offer you my grateful thanks but I did not do a very good job of protecting the wood from the east wind and look at the devastation now,' said Rahh, looking all around himself.

'Yes, Lord, but the east wind is not an animal like Red Fox but a great spirit that comes to bring change when it is needed,' said the brown creature.

'You are a wise creature,' said Rahh. 'What is your name?'

'I am Lepp. I live on the edge of the stream in the south of the woodland and these are many friends of yours who have come to see you with news of your friend,' said Lepp.

'Welcome, then,' said Rahh to all of them looking across their faces with a greeting in his eyes. 'How can I entertain you? Would you eat some grass and berries with me?'

'Lord, it is a sad day for the woodland and for all of us for we bring you sorry news of your friend. We fear there will be no more beautiful music in our woodland,' said Lepp. He stood aside and some other small creatures stepped forward. Between them they held out to Rahh some dried leaves, rolled carefully, one inside the other.

'We found these, Lord, and knew that you must see them but it is uncomfortable for us and also for you,' said Lepp.

Rahh took the roll of leaves and opened it carefully. Inside lay an array of red and brown feathers. He felt a jolt in his heart. A great wave of grief came upon him and he sank to the floor.

'We are so very sorry to bring this message to you, Lord, but the spirits of the great healers asked that we do so,' said Lepp.

Rahh could not find words at first, he just sat slumped and overwhelmed by his sensitive feelings. 'Oh, this cannot be. No, this cannot be. I thought that he would fly high into the invisibility and be blown over the tops of the woodland and then return as the east wind departed,' he said.

'We did not find his body, Lord,' said Lepp. 'It could be that he escaped with only losing a few feathers.'

'Yes, Lepp, you are right. This does not mean that he is not with us any longer. He may yet return, but at the moment I must lie down for a while and feel the truth of my feelings. Will you all please come to me at the next Great Light when it reaches its highest point in the blue?' asked Rahh.

Lepp looked at the others and they all agreed in a low tone that they would come. Rahh placed his paw in front of Lepp and Lepp placed his paw upon it signifying that a bond of deep friendship had been offered and accepted between them.

'Thank you. Now I must rest,' said Rahh.

He turned and took the feathers with him into the burrow. He went straight to his sleeping chamber and placed them beneath a soft pillow of dried grass and laid his head down upon them.

Rahh felt the darkness around him. He felt the desolation that he had felt so many times in the past when the heart-pain had dragged him to the ground. He lay for a long time just feeling his feelings.

Too soon the Great Light would come and he knew that it was a new dawn and that he would have to begin life again. All was changed and all was changing.

He drifted into the rabbit sleep and was soon in the dream-time where he was bounding down a hillside joyfully and then headfirst into a new burrow. Deep underground was the most beautiful music that he had ever heard and then a voice shouting out, 'Where have you been you jumping gerbil? I have been waiting here for lifetimes for you. You are the slowest hopper upon the Earth and even the Greatest of all Great Spirits would not wait for you!'

Rahh was uplifted by the music and laughed at the voice that he knew so well. 'I am here,' he shouted down the burrow. 'I am here, Fuff. I am sorry I was late but I had many lessons to learn along the way.'

'Well, now you are here I must leave because I have important work to do with some creatures of the invisibility that have a fear of flying. Can you believe it, rabbit?' asked Fuff, 'Birds with a fear of flying!'

'Now, take care Rahh. I have placed this music in your heart so that you will always hear me. I will not be far away perhaps just over the hill, or just over the hill into the next life. Try to remember, Rahh, there is no beginning and there is no end, there are only the circles. Only the Circles of Light.'

Rahh awoke to the sound of many small voices at the entrance to his burrow.

'Oh my whiskers,' he said to himself. 'Is the Great Light already high in the blue?'

He brushed his face with his paws, straightened his fur and hopped up to the entrance of the burrow. All the creatures from yesterday were there and also two feathered creatures with blue caps on their heads. They all went quiet when Rahh emerged from his hole in the ground.

'Ah, good morning,' said Rahh. 'Is the Great Light at its highest already?'

Lepp stepped forward and said, 'Yes, Lord. It has already passed the high point and we wondered if you might be unwell?'

'Thank you for your concern, but I was deeply taken into the dreamtime on a great journey and was not allowed to wake up. But I am with you now,' said Rahh, lifting his whiskers to the blue to show them he was happy to see them, and continued.

'Good morning friends. I would like to thank you for the great and courageous thing you did yesterday by bringing me the coat of my friend. It is good to know that at least a part of him is close to me. Although I will miss the sound of his music as the Great Light rises into the blue each cycle. Let us hope that he soon returns to us,' said Rahh. 'I would like to first invite you into my burrow. Please follow me.'

There was a ripple of excitement that ran through all the

creatures present. They were to be invited into the Lord's burrow. How wonderful and interesting to see the mysteries of the Lord's home.

Lepp lifted his nose to them to be calm and courteous and they all quietened down a little. They followed Rahh into the burrow, past the sleeping chamber that was still warm and to a small tunnel.

'I would like you all to go into this tunnel and bring out some food. It was gifted to me at the time that I frightened Red Fox away and it is now ready to be eaten. Today we will feast together to bond our friendship,' said Rahh.

'Now be sure to carry as much as you can. Do not be shy. This food is for sharing between all of us. Perhaps you will go first,' said Rahh to a small furry creature.

One at a time each creature entered the tunnel and came out with some food, then took it to the surface. Eventually, they had all come above ground again where they piled the food high and formed a circle around it. Rahh sat at one side of the circle and Lepp at the other.

'Dear friends,' said Rahh. 'I thank you for having the courage to speak of difficult things. My friend came to me in the dreamtime and he placed his music in my heart so I will forever know that he is close to me, even though I may not be able to see him at present beneath the Great Light.'

'At times we must all be lonely or alone so that we can learn about those feelings but today is a day of celebration for I have made many new friends. It was friends like you who brought to me all this food after Red Fox's fear made him run from our woodlands never to return. So, it brings me great joy to share this with you. Today we eat together as friends for by the next rising of the Great Light we cannot tell what fortunes will be ours or what fates await us. So, dear friends, please eat your fill and if we need more then enter my burrow and bring what you need.

Let us be filled with the joy of food and give thanks to the Great Light for blessing us with his presence,' said Rahh.

The creatures looked to Lepp who appeared to speak for them all and he nodded that they may proceed.

'Thank you Lord,' said Lepp. 'We are blessed to have you with us.'

Rahh smiled and took some berries to his lips. The bitterness suddenly reminded him of the berries that the wood mice once brought to him. He burst out laughing at the memory and the creatures all looked to him to see what was so funny.

Rahh then told them the story of how he was once such a foolish rabbit that he tried to enter the long rabbit sleep but the wood mice had saved him with berries such as these. They all laughed at the way Rahh told the story of how he thought he was being eaten by creatures unknown until he could once more open his eyes to see the wood mice feeding him. He made his new friends laugh as he acted out the great event of his near death experience.

The Great Light smiled down upon the creatures of the Earth. The great healers bowed their heads and watched the joy of the group of friends as they filled their bellies. And Rahh felt the faintest whisper of the wind spirit blowing through his whiskers again.

'Yes,' he thought.

'This is the bitterness that she spoke of. My friend has gone.'

49

The Pain of Love

After they had shared the food together the Great Light began to sink low. The cycles were getting shorter and the cold soon came. All the creatures came up to Rahh individually and placed a paw upon his as a sign of friendship. Lepp spoke eloquently about the creamy white moon that would soon pass through the wood and awaken their emotions and memories of the past. All the creatures listened carefully to Lepp's words and then they bid Rahh a good evening and left.

Rahh sat for a while watching the light fade and then went into his burrow. He could smell so many different aromas from the creatures who had visited his home this day and was happy for them all in that they seemed to have such a great creature to speak for them in Lepp.

Rahh set to tidying his sleeping chamber and considered that he must fetch some fresh bedding for the long period of the white lands that would visit soon. The following day he did just that, bringing fresh dry grass that would keep him warm.

The white lands arrived and the cold was intense. Many of the creatures slept for the whole of the cycle of short days and did not stir until the warmth of the Great Light again came to visit.

Rahh didn't really see anyone for a long time and spent his waking time thinking and wondering about many things. In some ways this had been a tough and painful life but at the same time it had been filled with the richness of great friendships. There had been deep, dark times where he had been overwhelmed with the pain of loss and other times where he had laughed and loved in the company of a great friend.

Rahh began to wonder why those who brought him the most love were also the ones that brought him the most pain when they left him. Yes, he could see the relationship between love and pain. It brought back Golden Rabbit's words to him.

'Is it painful, Rahh?' asked Golden Rabbit. 'Does it hurt inside?'

'Yes,' said Rahh. 'Why do I hurt so much? What is happening to me?'

Golden Rabbit said, 'You are Becoming.'

'What am I becoming?' asked Rahh.

'You are becoming filled with light, and as the light emerges from deep within your heart, the pain can be terrible.'

Rahh began to think about the light and the pain and realised that light and love were the same thing and both brought pain into the body when you experienced them deeply.

One day when it was particularly cold outside and the white lands were extremely bitter, Rahh took out the roll of leaves and opened it to look at Fuff's feathers. He touched them with his paw and immediately heard Fuff's music in his heart.

'What madness is this,' he thought, as the beautiful music brought tears to his eyes and great pain into his body. 'How can something as beautiful as this music cause me so much pain?'

Upon that thought, Fuff's voice spoke to him, as if from within his heart. 'Rahh, it is the pain of love from the music of love. It is the pain of love from all the stars in the heavens that bathe your life during the dark time. It is the pain of love from the great spirit of love that lights all the lights everywhere. The more you become love, the more you feel the pain of transformation from emptiness into love. The pain is part of your becoming.'

Rahh heard his own unspoken question. 'What am I becoming in all this pain?'

'You are becoming love, Rahh,' Fuff's voice answered him.

'You are becoming Love.'

Rahh fell to the floor, clutching Fuff's feathers to his heart with the tears pouring from his reddened eyes onto his paws. The pain took him deeply inside of himself and after much inner struggle he entered the rabbit sleep.

It was just another wave of love overcoming him.

It was just another day on his journey into becoming.

50

The Warm Cycle

It seemed to Rahh that he had been in the darkness for too many cycles of the Great Light and that he had not felt a ray of warmth or the sound of anything comforting for a long, long time.

As he hopped out of his burrow this morning though, there was a new energy in the wood. He could feel the buds swelling upon the trees and preparing themselves for bursting sometime soon.

There was also a sense of joy which seemed to be emanating from everywhere. As Rahh looked around he realised that mother was waking all the creatures that move freely on legs and all of the great beings that reach upwards from roots. His thoughts suddenly sprang to wondering if there were any new shoots of sweet, wet grass and his whiskers sprang upwards as his nose sniffed the warming invisibility.

'I will look,' said Rahh to himself as he took a deep breath to fill his fur. 'I will look for new green shoots.'

Rahh felt the energy inside him. This was the power of mother bringing life to a new warming cycle and all was filled with the energy of joy.

Within a few cycles of the Great Light, indeed there were signs of fresh green shoots appearing and within a few more cycles there was enough to make a decent sweet grassy breakfast, which filled Rahh with the new growing energy.

The Great Light was stretching out and rising higher and after many more cycles had passed life was beginning to rush into all of the veins in all life within the wood. As all this new life was rising to perfection, Rahh was aware of a growing stirring in his heart.

One morning, as he sat outside his burrow as the Great Light was just rising, he was listening to his heart to try to fathom what this stirring feeling was. From time to time he heard Fuff's music in there but also some rabbit fear and a great desire to eat the sweetest breakfast grass that any rabbit had ever eaten.

As he contemplated where he might find such grass a warm breeze floated gently through his whiskers. His ears pricked up and he turned his back to the Great Light and looked into the west.

There was suddenly a great feeling of being alone again. Even though he had friends he knew that he was truly on his own. He was on a journey through life whilst his friends were merely getting on with it. They were different, even though they were all lovely creatures and happy in their own way. They were not driven by the forces of the mother and father in the heart as he was.

He knew this warm breeze. It was the wind spirit, the courteous wind, the divine feminine wind that always helped him and sometimes brought change. It was time to change again – but how and why? The answers would no doubt come to him soon.

At the rising of the next Great Light, the new energy in the wood was much stronger and the words of Fuff came back to Rahh about the buds bursting into life. The children of the forest, he had called them, opening into the most wonderful expression of love.

And how the healers offered the promise of life each day through their waves of invisibility that wafted into your nose and mouth, filling you with that promise, but that it was up to you to make life out of that promise.

Soon it would be time for the leaves to open. Already the buds were bursting with energy and sticky with the juice of mother's love. Again Rahh felt a wisp of warmth on the breeze. The western wind spirit was getting restless and he could feel her strongly in his whiskers.

That night as he slept the spirit of the west wind took him into the dreamtime. She called softly into his ears, 'RRRaaahhhhhhh, it is time to move. It is time for you to wander upon the influence of your great spirit. It will be hard to leave this safe place that you have created for yourself but as the Great Cloak of Emerald Green opens its loving heart to all creatures, that will be your time to journey. That will be your time to follow your path once more into the unknown.'

Rahh drifted into wakefulness in a peaceful way. His first thought was that he didn't want to go anywhere, then he asked himself why he was even feeling that he was leaving. Suddenly, he sat up, his ears upright and alert. His whiskers were twitching; he realised that he had been in the dreamtime but it was different. It wasn't a dream. It was a message. Soon he would need to leave this burrow.

Fuff's words came back again. 'As each leaf unfolds they join together in the song of love, which forms the great cloak of the healers. The leaves are also the colour of love, which is green. It is the same colour as the light around your heart, Rahh. So when you look into the great healers of the forest they show you that they bring forth love into the world through their wonderfully coloured cloak. Also, you can see the colour of love in every blade of sweet grass that you eat in your morning breakfast.'

Rahh hopped to the burrow entrance with sweet breakfast grass on his mind as well as Fuff's other words.

It had been a long winter underground. The tears, the memories and the pain of love. But now this new energy was warming him. The sweet, wet morning grass was warming him and the rising Great Light was warming him.

Yes, he would be ready when the children of the forest could hold in the power of love no longer.

51

The Wandering

As the Great Light stayed longer in the blue the other animals in the wood were emerging. Rahh had spoken with Lepp at some length from time to time about his journey and Lepp had also spoken of his own. They knew that they were kindred spirits who had walked a similar path.

Lepp was indeed a wise creature from a long line of eloquent speakers who had served the woodland animals in times of difficulty and as a mediator. Lepp lived by the water and found that the different temperaments of the flow of water suited his heart. Sometimes the water was in flood and exciting, lifting his spirits and cleansing his mind and heart and at other times the flow was calming, allowing him to sit peacefully doing nothing.

Lepp knew that Rahh would leave soon on a journey, but he had said that he would return. Rahh had allowed Lepp to use his burrow and take whatever food was in the larder for a small gathering for all the creatures once he had left.

It was deep in the dark time when Rahh felt the first buds getting ready to burst at the next rising of the Great Light but he was already bright and awake. Mother had woken him to the tune that this was his time. Rahh kissed the feathers of Fuff and placed them beneath his pillow. Lepp had been instructed to take care of them until his return. He took one look around his sleeping chamber and hopped full of energy to the entrance of his burrow. The lights of Heaven were still bright and there was not yet a glow announcing the arrival of the Great Light.

'Now is my time,' he said to himself and began to walk the path that he and Fuff had first travelled together as they entered the wood. As he arrived at the edge of the wood there was the merest glow in the blue and he stepped into the ocean of green and hopped to the pool where he had first experienced the full power of the Dragon Fire in Fuff's transformation.

Rahh sat for a while and awaited the arrival of the Great Light. Its reflection was golden and blinding in the pool as he tried to look through the mirror into the heart of mother. He felt words coming up from his heart and spoke into the pool.

'Dear Mother, thank you for all of my life. Thank you for the light and the dark times. Thank you for the great friends that I have met upon my journey. I dedicate my life and all my thoughts to you and to Father and give you great thanks for all the wisdom that you have shared with me through the wonderful journey that you have guided me upon.'

'I am born of you, mother and Father. I am your essence, manifested and living upon the earth. You are in my heart and I am in yours for we are of one spirit, the Great Spirit of all that is. Thank you for all that you have made me.'

The words came spontaneously from Rahh's heart, tickling his whiskers as they flowed out of him. Once they had finished speaking he felt ready to move on. He looked back at the wood that had been most kind to his life and then blew a rabbit kiss into the pool.

He turned with the Great Light to his right hand side and began his journey to the north.

52

The Meeting

Rahh wandered through many cycles of the Great Light. He slept beneath bushes and sometimes curled up in a ball of grass. He slept many places that any normal rabbit would never dream of, but Rahh was not a normal rabbit; he was a rabbit who had chosen to leave home and follow the light of a great Golden Rabbit.

Here he was again in strange woodland and walking by himself, sometimes happy and full of joy in the warmth of the Great Light and sometimes sad and even in a dark place. He was a rabbit on his own.

During the last cycle of the Great Light he had found an old burrow that had not been used for some time and decided that he would rest for a while here. He was a little tired of not knowing where his journey was taking him.

He investigated the burrow and it was very cosy. There was even some dry grass that had been left and some roots of the healers above brought a good energy into the burrow. That night he sat and looked up into the brightly lit Heaven and felt each point of light falling into his heart. He thought to himself, 'The blue is full of love when the Great Light sleeps and that is why I can feel it in my heart.'

Rahh sat until his ears flopped and he almost fell over with sleepiness. At that point he went into the burrow, made himself comfortable and said a little prayer for all the friends he had known. He laid his head upon a small pillow and imagined that Fuff's feathers were beneath his head and then the dreamtime took him.

As he slept the dreamtime showed him images of his life. He was a tired rabbit. He was tired of the journey. He was tired with the learning and tired of the loneliness and the pain. The pain had drained his life-force, but somehow had made him strong too. In the dreamtime he was beneath the Great Light and small bunnies were all around him, looking at him and admiring him. The Great Light shone upon all their lives and was more golden than ever he had seen it. He could hear the most beautiful music he had ever heard and wished that Fuff was here to hear it too.

Just then a breeze came up behind him blowing softly between his ears and playfully tickling his whiskers. It was his old friend the wind spirit.

'RRRaaahhhhhh, rest your weary body, your weary heart, your weary life, for you have learned much. You have borne the journey of a saviour and you are filled with love and hope. Soon you will find peace and your friends will walk with you again. Let yourself go and surrender to your Mother and Father, and all will be well.'

The wind spirit continued on her journey and Rahh continued to watch himself sleeping until the vision faded.

As the dark time gave way to the rising of the Great Light, Rahh continued to lie in his burrow. He didn't want come out. He felt the weariness he had seen in the dreamtime and he felt a little fear of the unknown. But he was also hungry. His furry belly was speaking to him to eat a Light breakfast. He hadn't really eaten a Light breakfast for some time. He just went through the motions of eating without thinking consciously, which was contrary to what Golden Rabbit had taught him during so many breakfasts in the past.

Golden Rabbit's words echoed in his ears. 'Be aware, Rahh, of all things that you think and do. Be aware at all times and be wary.'

Rahh thought to himself that truly he had not been aware of anything these past weeks other than the pain in his belly from missing his friend Fuff. This morning there was twice the pain as he was becoming very aware of his hunger. Slowly he came out of the darkness of the burrow and into the light of the woodland. The feathered creatures were making music of a sort and for a moment he felt their joy in his heart; he lifted his weary eyes from the ground to see the green cloak of love covering everything with the invisibility and the promise of life.

There seemed to be Light in the wood this morning and his heart skipped at the thought that Golden Rabbit had returned, but then realised that the Great Light is near its zenith in the warm cycle and he was also late rising from his burrow. He looked around him but couldn't see any other creatures. He was definitely alone.

Suddenly he jumped in surprise that his body was hopping by itself and he was so deeply within his thoughts and feelings that he had been unaware. He found it quite funny, as if he was separate and observing himself hopping slowly through the wood.

'Well,' he thought to himself, forgetting his hunger and experiencing a new jolly feeling in his ears, 'I'll just see where this body of mine is taking me. I'll just follow it.'

By and by Rahh came to a small green glade where the Great Light shone through the cloak of the healers. He stopped and began to nibble some of the sweet grass, which was warming nicely as the day progressed. He remembered this place from long, long ago. It was familiar. As he ate and thought it came to him. This was where he had met Golden Rabbit on that morning when he left his family.

He suddenly found his thoughts going back all those years and wondering, for the first time really, how his brothers and sisters were. He remembered Golden Rabbit's words on that first day of the journey: 'They've already forgotten you.'

Again he realised how lonely he was inside. How empty, how so alone. These last days had been so up and down, joy then pain, happiness then grief, almost changing with each breath. Only a moment ago he was in the joy of watching where his body was taking him and now he had fallen into an old memory.

The warmth in the glade touched him again and he realised that his tummy was now full and he had forgotten to eat a Light breakfast and had just eaten grass instead, even though it was lovely.

His body began to slowly hop again but his whiskers were down as he drifted through the woodland. He seemed to be here and there at the same time, not happy not sad, but somewhere in between. He noted that his whiskers were down but his ears were up and this swamp of confused emotions and feelings made him chuckle at himself. Speaking aloud he said, 'I don't know whether I'm coming or going. I am just a confused rabbit!'

Suddenly, Rahh's ears pricked up as he heard the sound of young bunnies in the distance playing, their voices carrying on the breeze. He turned his ears this way and that whilst looking through the wood where he could see some splashes of light entering the shade. He hopped quietly towards the light and he could see the edge of the wood. Beyond lay neat green lawns, like those that he had played on as a young bunny himself.

He saw some older rabbits eating quietly and the young bunnies were running and dashing here and there in a playful dance, filled with joy.

Quietly he sat in the wood and watched for a long, long time. Memories were coming back to him: was this where he once lived and were those old rabbits his brothers and sisters? But they looked so old, their fur was grey and mottled. He wondered, did he look like that too?

As the Great Light in the blue rose to its highest point he realised that he must have sat for a long time, half watching, half remembering and wondering about his journey since he walked away from home with Golden Rabbit.

There was that old thorn in his side again making him wonder if he had made a big mistake. He had certainly been on a great journey, but watching this peaceful scene and hearing the joyful cries of the young bunnies made him wonder what might have been if he hadn't followed the Light of Golden Rabbit.

Upon that thought, Rahh was suddenly startled to see a young bunny sitting watching him. But as his eyes fell upon the bunny, it turned and ran. He sat upright to see where it had gone to.

'Mmm,' thought Rahh, 'I must have frightened the little fellow. Perhaps he was startled to see a strange rabbit in his woodland. I'd better move on.' As he turned to leave he heard some bunnies whispering behind him. He looked over his shoulder to see five young bunnies and two elder rabbits behind them all looking at him.

'Oh dear,' thought Rahh. 'I've really disturbed them now and they must want me to leave their woodland.' He said, 'I am sorry to disturb you. I shall leave your space and go back into the deep woodland immediately.'

'Please wait,' said one of the elder rabbits. 'Perhaps you can help us?'

Rahh turned to face them and lowered his whiskers to show respect and that he meant them no harm.

'How can I help you? I am sure that I don't know,' said Rahh.

'We have heard about you,' said one of the elder rabbits. 'Yes,' said the other elder rabbit and the young bunnies whispered amongst themselves excitedly.

'How can you have heard of me?' asked Rahh, surprised.

The elder rabbit spoke. 'It has been passed down in the Rabbit Law that one day a great Golden Rabbit came to the edge of our wood and around him was the greatest Golden Light, like that of the Great Light in the blue. It is said that he spoke to young bunnies and they were filled with joy from that day forward. It is true that all of our burrow is always full of joyful chatter, and when the young bunnies rise from their burrow with the Great Light, they dance upon the green carpet before eating breakfast grass.'

'And how do you think I can help you with this story?' asked Rahh.

The elder rabbit spoke again. 'We are blessed this day that you have returned to us, Golden Rabbit and filled our woodland again with your light. Many seasons and cycles have passed beneath the Great Light in the blue. The leaves have grown green and fresh and fallen to the ground, cool and brown many times and there are no rabbits living now that ever saw you before.'

He continued, 'Rabbits have birthed and rabbits have passed into the long rabbit sleep and the elders have passed down the Rabbit Law of when you came to our woodland long, long ago.'

'I am not Golden Rabbit,' said Rahh.

'But you fill the woodland with your Golden Light,' said the elder. 'You are just as the Rabbit Law said you were. You are a great Golden Rabbit. Look into our eyes and you will see your reflection.'

Rahh leaned forward and the little bunnies drew their heads back in fear. In the shiny, dark brown pools of their eyes, Rahh saw the reflection of a Golden Rabbit. He shone like the Great Light in the blue, illuminating everything around him. Rahh sat back with his ears pointing straight upwards. He looked at the group sitting before him, just as he had sat in a group looking at Golden Rabbit all those long years before.

By now many other rabbits from the burrow had gathered in Rahh's light and they were all enraptured waiting patiently for him to speak, whilst he continued to look into their eyes finding it difficult to believe what he saw in the reflection. He said, 'I am not the Golden Rabbit that came here once before. My name is Rahh.'

The rabbits sat up and looked at each other questioningly. The elder rabbit spoke again. 'Then The Rabbit Law is true, but it can't be so,' he said. 'It says that one of our family went with the Golden Rabbit and was never seen again. His name was Rahh.'

'I am Rahh, who left the burrow to go with the Golden Rabbit,' said Rahh.

[239]

'Rahh was the brother of our grandparents, which means that if you are the same Rahh, then you will have lived three rabbit lifetimes already – but you look so young and full of life.'

Rahh looked at them and with a smile said, 'It seems to be that way at times. It has been a very long journey.'

The elder rabbit asked, 'But how did you grow so large and so bright? You are much bigger than we are.'

Rahh replied, 'That in itself would take a rabbit lifetime to tell you and perhaps one day, when the warm cycles are very long, I will be happy to sit out under the sparkling heavens and do just that.'

The elder continued. 'If you are Rahh, then where is the Golden Rabbit that you left with all those years ago?'

Rahh answered as best as he could. 'There came a time when the Golden Rabbit had to leave and I was all alone in the deep, deep woodland. I felt lost and frightened, but Golden Rabbit had given me one instruction before leaving. She said: 'Remember, Rahh, you are never alone. You are Becoming.''

'Golden Rabbit was a great teacher. She taught me many things that ordinary rabbits do not know, but more than that, she took me on a journey into the truth of all that is and this truth was found in my own heart,' said Rahh.

The bunnies and the elders had crept forward a little to show respect for Rahh's words and begged to hear more of his story.

Rahh continued to tell them of his journey and as he spoke he felt the wisdom of Golden Rabbit speaking through him. Her light filled his heart and her words flowed over his tongue in a golden stream of joy that bathed the ears of those who were ready to hear them. The bunnies, older rabbits and elders were enthralled by the story and as the Great Light in the blue began to fall towards the earth, the dusk began to gather.

As Rahh continued telling his story he could see the light in their eyes becoming brighter and the reflection began to dazzle him. At the same moment, all those gathered shrank back a little, shading their eyes with their paws against the increasing intensity of the light.

Rahh saw the ears of the elders fall flat against their back and they put their chins between their paws.

And then a voice that was so familiar to Rahh softly spoke from behind him.

'And now, Rahh, you have become.'

'You have become a Golden Rabbit.'

53

The Audience

Rahh's heart burst open with joy as he looked behind him.

'Golden Rabbit!' he exclaimed.

'Yes, Rahh, it is I,' said Golden Rabbit.

'Where have you been? I thought I would never see you again.'

'I will tell you later,' said Golden Rabbit, 'but now I see you have an audience.'

Rahh looked back at the bunnies, the grown rabbits and the elders and said, 'Yes, Golden Rabbit. They were just telling me about the Rabbit Law, and how a great Golden Rabbit came into the woods one day – and they thought that I was you.'

Golden Rabbit stepped forward and stood next to Rahh. There was so much light in the woodland that the other rabbits were trembling with joy. They could see that this Golden Rabbit was much bigger than Rahh, and indeed, Rahh was bigger than they were. Again the Rabbit Law was true.

'Please may I see the faces of your students as they sit illuminated by your light, Rahh?' asked Golden Rabbit, looking at Rahh.

Rahh looked at Golden Rabbit, surprised. 'My students?' he said, 'but these are just rabbits from the garden yonder.'

Golden Rabbit said, 'Did they come to you in the darkness of the wood?'

'Yes,' said Rahh.

'Did they come because of your Light?'

'Yes,' said Rahh.

'Did they wish to hear your words?' asked Golden Rabbit.

'Yes,' said Rahh.

'Then they are your students, Rahh. Some may walk with you

for a moment or for a day and some may walk with you for your whole life, and they will be your companions as you show them the things that I have shown to you. You will pass on the knowledge and carry the light into their hearts and eventually some of them will become.'

'When you return to the deep woodland and the Field of Wonders you will not be alone, for at least one will follow you and if only one is ready, then only one will come to the light that you carry as a Golden Rabbit.'

The bunnies, rabbits and elders were watching and listening carefully to these two great Golden Rabbits speaking before them.

Rahh looked at the innocent bunnies, the worldly wise grown-ups and the elders.

An elder cleared his throat and lifted his whiskers. 'Please may I speak?' he asked.

The Golden Rabbits nodded, lowered their whiskers and remained respectfully silent.

'Our woodland has been filled with great light today. Probably the greatest morning since the ancient Rabbit Law was first spoken of. Today we have seen the truth of the Law and that you great Golden Rabbits have come to bless our burrows once again.'

'There was also other talk about the Law that was not as wholesome, but it needs to be spoken of now, with your permission.'

The elder rabbit waited and Golden Rabbit and Rahh nodded their heads to this request.

'It was said by some that the great Golden Rabbit had stolen Rahh and run with him into the dark wood, never to be seen again.'

The other rabbits mumbled and nodded and spoke as a group, 'Yes, it is said.'

'When I saw your light in our wood this morning, I knew that story could not be true because your light is full of beauty. Also, I see that you wear the white patch on your left paw, which is the mark of our burrow and so it must be true that you are Rahh.'

'This deep, deep wood that you speak of, and the Field of Wonders...Even though my years are long and I am probably not far from the long rabbit sleep, I would like to go with you to see them. I have been happy and joyful in this burrow all my life but perhaps it is time for an adventure.'

'If you are truly Rahh my ancestor who left this burrow to walk with the Great Golden Rabbit and you have returned today to show us that you have also become a Great Golden Rabbit yourself, then this is a journey that I am willing to take. It would only be a foolish rabbit or indeed a blind rabbit who would not wish to take such a journey by your side.'

There were nods and mumblings of agreement from some of the other rabbits.

Rahh looked at their radiant faces, illuminated by his light.

'I am Rahh who once ate the green grass of these lawns behind you, and I am the same Rahh who left to walk with Golden Rabbit. I am that Rahh who found my way back here this morning, not really knowing where I was hopping, but clearly my paws were guided to you. Yes, I am your ancestor and I am blessed to meet you all, my family.'

'The Great Light is already bowing to kiss his wife and so I must leave you now, but at the next rising of the Great Light I will return. Those of you who are ready may hop with me a while and hear some more of my story. It may be the beginning of a long journey for you, or it may be but a single cycle of the Great Light, and there is no promise that you will ever return to this burrow.'

'However, I will make you one promise that I can keep. It will be the promise that you will feel life.'

The rabbits sat up again and Golden Rabbit and Rahh bid them a good evening, turned and hopped into the wood.

Rahh followed Golden Rabbit as she made her way through

the long grass to the little glade where once they had stood together on that first day when Rahh was a young bunny.

Golden Rabbit stopped and turned to face Rahh and then spoke.

'Shall we eat of the green shoots in this glade together, Golden Rabbit Rahh, as once we did before, on that first day of your journey?'

Rahh felt the tears in his heart as Golden Rabbit called him Golden Rabbit. He felt the deep exhaustion of the journey and he felt the relief of realising that he had arrived at his destiny. He began to feel the becoming as it shone out through his whiskers to fill the invisibility with love.

'Oh yes please, Golden Rabbit. Suddenly I am so hungry I could eat a whole Field of Wonders.'

54

The Greatest Gift

Rahh was always hungry when he had a burning question.

Golden Rabbit's whiskers were wet from the grass as she nibbled. She could sense Rahh's burning question but he was so hungry that he could not speak.

She said, 'Rahh. I sense your burning question and your hunger will not go away until you blow it out through your whiskers.'

'Where did you go, Golden Rabbit? I thought you had been taken by Red Fox. I never knew if you were safe or had entered the long rabbit sleep.'

'Rahh, do you remember when first you stepped into this green circle all those years ago?'

'Yes,' said Rahh.

'Do you recall that you were the only bunny that could look into my eyes?'

'Yes,' said Rahh.

'Do you recall what I said to you?'

'You said, 'Show me your courage,'' said Rahh.

'I also said to you, your courage is in your heart and it is reaching out to the Light that is inside me. That is why your name is Rahh, because you have the courage of the lion and your heart shines like the Great Light in the blue,' said Golden Rabbit.

'Yes, I recall,' said Rahh.

'Well, there is more to just a name, Rahh, and names are given through the heart of the mother who can feel the child within her belly. There was once a greater Golden Rabbit than I; perhaps the greatest ever. This rabbit came in ancient times and walked upon pastures green, like we have done. The heart of this rabbit was full of love and he spread the fire of love upon the earth and he still guards it until it is awake from where he now dwells.'

'That fire is the light in your heart, Rahh and the greatest rabbit has now awakened it. Your name tells those with eyes to see who you are. You are Ra, the God of the Great Light in the blue with the Holy Heart that roars like the lion full of courage. Rahh, with the heart that is fully illuminated by the Light of the greatest rabbit ever to walk upon Mother's breast.'

'When the west wind calls your name, she whispers, *RRRaaahhhhhh*. She tells you who you are, like this: *RRRaaa* – God of the Great Light. *hhhhhh* – Holy Heart, Holy Heart, Holy Heart.'

'You were sent here to this life to become a Golden Rabbit, and I was instructed to be your guide and teacher. Your mother knew that you were special and different from your first squeaking sounds. She knew that one day you would have to leave the burrow and that she might never see you again. The day she saw my Golden Light in the woodland, she knew that the Greatest Rabbit to ever walk upon these pastures green had sent me for you and that she would have to give you up and let you go. She cried a thousand rabbit tears as you followed me into the wood. That is how I knew your name on that first day, when we stood in this circle together, Rahh. Your name was written upon every tear that spilled from her heart.'

'It was the first Golden Rabbit of ancient times who gave you your name through your mother. It was written on your heart in light. This is Rahh, the Shining One with a Holy Heart.'

'We are in new times, Rahh, and the twinkling lights of the heavens are changing and moving quickly. Other rabbits are hearing the call of the light in their hearts and it will seek the light of a Shining One to help it to awaken. You are now ready to guide them into light, Rahh.'

Rahh had been listening very closely to Golden Rabbit. She was always full of wisdom and surprises.

'Now, what about your question, Rahh?' said Golden Rabbit.

'Why did you leave me, Golden Rabbit?' he said.

'I know the pain that you must have felt, Rahh. It caused me great pain too, to leave you, as you are like my own whiskers you are so close to me, but there is a gift that the Greatest Golden Rabbit from ancient times gives to us all when we are ready to receive it. It is the Greatest Gift that you can receive in life.'

Golden Rabbit waited a moment to ensure that all of her words were going into Rahh's heart. 'This gift opens the final petals for the Light to burst out of your heart and call to those who are ready to see and hear it.'

'You will also have to leave those you love at some point on this great path and you then learn to see the great gift as it opens in those whom you love.'

'Please tell me what this great gift is, Golden Rabbit?' cried Rahh.

'What happened to you, Rahh, when you realised that I was not there anymore?'

'I was empty, but at the same time I was filled with the greatest pain I ever felt. My fur was full of terrible, terrible pain and my tears ran for many cycles. I stayed in my burrow and was filled with a darkness that was unspeakable. The white lands of bitterness took me close to the long rabbit sleep and I was ready to enter that doorway. Even the rabbit of death came to my burrow. I was broken. The pain was so great. I never wanted to come out of the burrow again.'

Golden Rabbit said, 'That pain is the greatest gift, Rahh.'

'How is such great pain a great gift, Golden Rabbit?' asked Rahh.

'It is the gift of a broken heart,' said Golden Rabbit.

'The heart must be smashed so hard that the pain almost kills you. Through the smashed and broken heart the light of the greatest rabbit to ever walk upon these pastures green begins to flood out from your centre and into the world. The Light transforms you and you feel the pain of love as it illuminates everything within your fur that is not light. After some time the light begins to heal your broken heart, but not before it has established itself so strongly in your life that it changes you forever. There is no going back and there is no choice.'

'At the moment the heart breaks and the light floods out, it illuminates all of your darkness, which then overwhelms you. You have no idea that Light is emerging within you, until one day like today, you see yourself reflected in the eyes of others. Only then can you see the great Golden Rabbit that you have become.'

Rahh was silent in respect of Golden Rabbit's words. He allowed their wisdom to enter his heart and they sat for a short while in each other's light, just bathing.

'What happens now, Golden Rabbit? Will you come back to your old burrow? Will we travel together again and go to the Field of Wonders and eat a Light breakfast?'

'Yes, Rahh, for now I will be with you again. There will be a time for me to leave but you will know when that time is coming and will be able to adjust to it; it will not hurt in the same way. But still, you will feel that a part of you is being torn away inside when I go and that piece I will save for when we meet again on the other side of the long, still rabbit sleep.'

'The rabbits from your burrow will be waiting for you in the morning. It is your time to lead them into the darkness of the inner wood. You will be their guide. You will hold their paws when they tremble. You will pour your light into their hearts and make the water of life flow from their eyes, and one day, some of them will stand beside you as Golden Rabbits, born of the line of Rahh. Then truly they will know who you are and the inner journey you have made in order to carry such a great Light.'

'Now Rahh, shall we go to our burrow and share some soft, warm grass for the dark time?

'Oh yes please, Golden Rabbit,' said Rahh.

'Rahh, there is no beginning, there is no end, there is only the Circle of Light. Today you have completed your first circle and seen your love reflected in the eyes of others.'

'As we rise from our beds with the next Great Light let us

celebrate together with some breakfast grass. Let us take the emerald jewels into our mouths and taste the light that Mother and Father lay before us and breathe the promise of life in the invisibility.'

'Let us celebrate how you took the promise of life deep within you and turned it into gold.'

'And most importantly, let us celebrate that you have been seen and recognised for what you have become.'

'A Golden Rabbit.'

First published by David Ashworth, 2018
Whitchurch, Shropshire SY13 4EH
email: dave@davidashworth.com
www.davidashworth.com

Illustrations by Sue Edwards

Set in Adobe Garamond Premier Pro
Typesetting by Christian Brett

ISBN 978-1-7293253-0-8

Sign up to Golden Rabbit's Teachings on Facebook:
Facebook.com/GoldenRabbitWisdom/
www.Golden-Rabbit.uk

Also by David Ashworth

Dancing with the Devil as you Channel in the Light
The Keys of Transformation
VISION
The Vision Journey (movie)
Ocean of Emotion
Revealing Truth (DVD)
The Yellow Kite
The Princess and the Bear (poetry)
Fairy Stories – Encounters with Nature Spirits
The Shaman's Journey – A Guided Meditation (CD)

Printed in Poland
by Amazon Fulfillment
Poland Sp. z o.o., Wrocław

54633987R00155